THE RIVER RHONE CYCLE ROUTE

FROM THE ALPS TO THE MEDITERRANEAN

by Mike Wells

JUNIPER HOUSE, MURLEY MOSS,
OXENHOLME ROAD, KENDAL, CUMBRIA LA9 7RL
www.cicerone.co.uk

© Mike Wells 2023
Second edition 2023
ISBN: 978 1 78631 082 8
First edition 2016
ISBN: 978 1 85284 755 5

Printed in China on responsibly sourced paper on behalf of Latitude Press Ltd
A catalogue record for this book is available from the British Library.
All photographs are by the author unless otherwise stated.

Route mapping by Lovell Johns www.lovelljohns.com
Contains OpenStreetMap.org data © OpenStreetMap
contributors, CC-BY-SA. NASA relief data courtesy of ESRI

Updates to this guide

While every effort is made by our authors to ensure the accuracy of guide-books as they go to print, changes can occur during the lifetime of an edition. Any updates that we know of for this guide will be on the Cicerone website (www.cicerone.co.uk/1082/updates), so please check before planning your trip. We also advise that you check information about such things as transport, accommodation and shops locally. Even rights of way can be altered over time. We are always grateful for information about any discrepancies between a guidebook and the facts on the ground, sent by email to updates@cicerone.co.uk or by post to Cicerone, Juniper House, Murley Moss, Oxenholme Road, Kendal, LA9 7RL.

Register your book: To sign up to receive free updates, special offers and GPX files where available, register your book in your Cicerone library at www.cicerone.co.uk.

Front cover: Yvoire castle and harbour (Stage 6)

CONTENTS

Distance marker on riverside cycle track in Laveyron (Stage 13)

LA SOURCE - 577km ▶
◀ 235km - LA MER

PREFACE TO THE SECOND EDITION

In France the planning of long-distance cycle routes is a national and regional government responsibility. However, the implementation of these plans by building the infrastructure is delegated to *départements* (counties), some of which are quicker than others in getting the job done. When the first edition was written, 75 per cent of the ViaRhôna route was definite and waymarked. The rest existed as proposed routings and these were used as the base for the guide. This was particularly the case in the départements of Isère, Rhône, Vaucluse and Gard, plus the city of Lyon. Subsequently, in a number of places the route finally chosen, provided with infrastructure and waymarked did not correspond with the initial proposals. This second edition incorporates all the new sections that have been completed in the last five years and the route is now 95 per cent complete. As a result the long detour following Swiss Rhone route R1 around the north side of Lake Geneva is no longer necessary and this edition follows a route along the south (French) shore of the lake.

There are still a few short provisional sections where roads have to be followed, particularly along the south side of Lake Geneva (Haute-Savoie), before and after Lyon (Rhône), and from Avignon to Arles (Gard). These sections are fully described in this guide, although they may change as the final pieces are put into place. As these sections are completed, details will be posted on the 'updates' page of the Cicerone website.

STAGE SUMMARY TABLE

Stage	Start	Finish	Distance	Waymarking	Page
1	Furka Belvédère	Brig (Naters), Rottubrigga bridge	55.5km	R1	48
2	Brig (Naters), Rottubrigga bridge	Sierre/Siders, Rue du Bourg	41km	R1	62
3	Sierre/Siders, Rue du Bourg	Martigny, Branson bridge	44.5km	R1	70
4	Martigny, Branson bridge	St Gingolph, boat pier	44.5km	R1/R46	78
5	St Gingolph, boat pier	Thonon-les-Bains, Port de Rives	28.5km	ViaRhôna	109
6	Thonon-les-Bains, Port de Rives	Geneva, Pl de St Gervais	45.5km	ViaRhôna/R46	116
7	Geneva, Pl de St Gervais	Seyssel, Pl de l'Orme	59km	R1/ViaRhôna	126
8	Seyssel, Pl de l'Orme	Champagneux, dam	53km	ViaRhôna	136
9	Champagneux, dam	Lagnieu, bridge	63km	ViaRhôna	144
10	Lagnieu, bridge	Lyon, pont de la Guillotière bridge	64.5km	ViaRhôna	153
11	Lyon, pont de la Guillotière bridge	Vienne, Ste Colombe quay	35.5km	ViaRhôna	164
12	Vienne, Ste Colombe quay	Sablons, bridge	33km	ViaRhôna	173
13	Sablons, bridge	Tournon-sur-Rhône, bridge	36km	ViaRhôna	178
14	Tournon-sur-Rhône, bridge	Valence, monumental fountain	24km	ViaRhôna	184
15	Valence, monumental fountain	Le Pouzin, roundabout	33.5km	ViaRhôna	189

Stage	Start	Finish	Distance	Waymarking	Page
16	Le Pouzin, roundabout	Montélimar, Pracomtal bridge	30km	ViaRhôna	196
17	Montélimar, Pracomtal bridge	Pont-St Esprit, Le Bout-du-Pont	41km	ViaRhôna	204
18	Pont-St Esprit, Le Bout-du-Pont	Avignon, Centre station	56.5km	ViaRhôna	212
19	Avignon, Centre station	Arles, Bvd Clemenceau	58.5km	ViaRhôna	222
20	Arles, Bvd Clemenceau	Port-St Louis-du-Rhône, Tour St Louis	43km	ViaRhôna	231
		Total	**890km**		
		Switzerland	**226.5km**		
		France	**663.5km**		

Using route north of Lake Geneva

Stage	Start	Finish	Distance	Waymarking	Page
5A	Le Bouveret, bridge	Morges, Temple de Morges	50km	R1/R46	86
6A	Morges, Temple de Morges	Geneva, Pl de St Gervais	58km	R1/R46	101
		Total	**917.5km**		
		Switzerland	**312.5km**		
		France	**605km**		

A statue of Archangel Michael sits atop a limestone ridge overlooking the Rhone near Viviers (Stage 17)

TWELVE-DAY SCHEDULE

Day	Start	Finish	Stage	Distance
1	Furka Belvédère	Brig	1	55.5km
2	Brig	Martigny	2–3	85.5km
3	Martigny	Évian-les-Bains	4–5	61km
4	Évian-les-Bains	Geneva	5–6	57.5km
5	Geneva	Chanaz	7–8	81.5km
6	Chanaz	Montalieu-Vercieu	8–9	80km
7	Montalieu-Vercieu	Lyon	9–10	78km
8	Lyon	St Vallier	11–13	87km
9	St Vallier	Le Pouzin	13–15	75km
10	Le Pouzin	Pont d'Esprit	16–17	71km
11	Pont d'Esprit	Beaucaire	18–19	95km
12	Beaucaire	Port-St Louis	19–20	63km
			Total	**890km**
			Average	**74km per day**

The old Belvédère hotel is high on the Furkapass (Stage 1)

INTRODUCTION

The shore of Lake Geneva in Montreux is lined with floral displays (Stage 5A)

Running from the Swiss Alps to the Mediterranean Sea, the valley of the river Rhone has for many centuries been one of the great communication links of western Europe. The Romans conquered Gaul by marching their legions up the lower Rhone valley from the sea, while over 1850 years later the French Emperor Napoléon took his army the other way by using the upper valley as a route to invade Italy. For modern-day French families the lower Rhone valley is the *route du soleil* (route to the sun) which they follow every summer to reach vacation destinations in the South of France. For much of its length the river is followed by railways, roads and motorways carrying goods to and from great Mediterranean ports such as Marseille and Genoa.

In addition to being a major transport artery, the Rhone valley is host to an attractive long-distance cycle route that makes its way for 890km from the high Alps to the Rhone delta using a mixture of traffic-free tracks and country roads. As it follows a great river, the route is mostly downhill.

After many years of planning and construction, the Rhone Cycle Route is almost complete, making it a viable means of cycling from central Switzerland to the South of France in a generally quiet environment by using two waymarked national cycle trails: the Swiss Rhone Route R1 and the French ViaRhôna. These have been adopted by the ECF (European Cyclists' Federation) as EuroVelo route EV17. This guide breaks the route into 20 stages, averaging 45km in length. A reasonably fit cyclist, riding 74km per day, should be able to complete the route in 12 days. Allowing for a gentler ride with time for sightseeing on the way, the route can be cycled in a fortnight by most cyclists.

The Swiss Rhone Route R1, part of the extensive Swiss Veloland network (www.veloland.ch), runs from the river's source near the summit of the Furkapass for 186km to the Swiss/French border at St Gingolph on the shore of Lake Geneva. En route it follows a deep glacial valley with snow-capped mountains rising on both sides.

After crossing into France, the ViaRhôna is followed firstly along the south side of Lake Geneva, then through a deep limestone gorge between the Jura mountains and the Savoy Alps. After passing through Lyon, France's second city, it turns south through a wider gorge along the geological fault line between the Alps and Massif Central to reach the Mediterranean. The main cities along this valley – Lyon, Valence and Arles – have history going back to the Iron Age and there is much evidence of Roman civilisation including the ruins of temples, arena, amphitheatres and bath-houses. Other cities, particularly Vienne and Avignon, were important medieval religious centres with large cathedrals and clerical palaces.

Vineyards of Lavaux cover the lakeside slopes between Vevey and Lausanne (Stage 5A)

ViaRhôna (www.viarhona.com) is a dedicated cycle track being built to French *voie verte* standards (traffic-free, 3m wide, asphalt surface) all the way from the Swiss border to the sea. While this is about 95 per cent complete, there are sections, particularly in Haut Savoie south of Lake Geneva (Stages 5/6), before and after Lyon (Stages 10/11), and between Avignon and Arles (Stage 19) where quiet country roads need to be used. Heavy traffic is only encountered on one stage, when heading south out of Lyon (Stage 11). This can be avoided if desired by taking the train for 36km from Lyon to Vienne.

Throughout the route there are a wide variety of places to stay, from campsites through to youth hostels, guest houses and small family run hotels, all the way up to some of the world's greatest five-star hotels. Local tourist offices in almost every town will help you find accommodation and often book it for you. It is the same for food and drink, with eating establishments in every price range including two of France's most famous (and expensive!) three-star Michelin restaurants (Paul Bocuse near Lyon and Maison Pic in Valence). In both Switzerland (where the birthplace and grave of César Ritz is passed on Stage 1) and France, where culinary skills are in evidence in almost all establishments, even the smallest local restaurants offer home-cooked meals using quality local ingredients. If you like wine, there are plentiful opportunities to sample local vintages in both countries as the route passes through the Swiss wine-producing areas of Valais, Lavaux and La Côte, and many French ones including Côte-Rôtie, Condrieu, Hermitage, Côtes du Rhône and Châteauneuf-du-Pape.

The Rhone Cycle Route passes through two countries. Although both countries speak French (albeit only partly so in Switzerland) they have very different histories, culture and ways of government.

Switzerland

Switzerland is a federation of 26 *cantons* (federal states). It was founded in 1291 (on 1 August, now celebrated as Swiss national day), although some of west Switzerland through which the route passes did not join the federation until 1803. Modern Switzerland is regarded as a homogenous, prosperous and well-organised country, but this was not always the case.

Roman occupation

Before the arrival of the Romans in 15BC, the land north of the Alps that is modern Switzerland was inhabited by the Helvetii, a Gallic Iron Age tribe. More than 400 years of Roman rule left its mark with many archaeological remains. During the fourth century AD, the Romans came under increasing pressure from Germanic tribes from the north and by AD401

13

had withdrawn their legions from the region.

Early Swiss history

After the Romans departed, two tribes occupied the area: the Burgundians in the west and Alemanni in the east. This division lives on 1600 years later in the division between the French and German speaking parts of Switzerland. The Burgundian territory south of Lake Geneva passed through a number of hands before becoming part of Savoy in 1003. North of the lake, the territory became divided between a number of city states, all part of the Holy Roman Empire. The Alemanni territory became part of Berne, also within the Holy Roman Empire. Expansionist Berne joined the Swiss Federation in 1353 and gradually absorbed all the city states (except Geneva), leaving Berne and Savoy facing each other across the lake. Most of the fortifications in western Switzerland are either Bernese or Savoyard and reflect regular tensions between these countries. Both were feudal states with a large number of peasants ruled over by noble elites.

Napoleonic era

This division ended when French revolutionary forces invaded Savoy (1792) and Napoléon invaded Geneva and Berne (1798), bringing the whole region temporarily under French control. Napoléon re-established a Swiss Confederation in 1803, separating Valais from Savoy and breaking up Berne into smaller cantons including Vaud. The feudal structure was abolished and the cantons in this confederation were set up with governments based on democratic principles. After Napoléon's fall (1815), the Congress of Vienna gave Savoy to the kingdom of Sardinia, a nation that already controlled neighbouring Piedmont in northern Italy. This congress also recognised Swiss neutrality.

Nineteenth-century Switzerland

For most of the 19th century, Switzerland remained one of Europe's poorest countries, relying upon agriculture with very little industry or natural resources. The coming of railways that enabled rich visitors from northern Europe to visit the Alps and the attraction of clean air and medical facilities for those with consumption and bronchitis started to lift the Swiss economy. The development of hydroelectric generation gave Switzerland plentiful cheap energy and spurred the growth of engineering businesses. Swiss banks in Zürich and Geneva, with a policy of secrecy and a reputation for trust, attracted funds from foreign investors who wished to avail themselves of these benefits.

Modern-day prosperity

Although neutral and not involved in the fighting, Switzerland suffered badly during the First World War when foreign visitors were unable to reach the country and markets for its engineering products dried up. Post-war recovery was led by the banking sector. Political and economic turmoil in Russia and Germany boosted Swiss bank receipts. Swiss neutrality made it the obvious location for multinational bodies such as the League of Nations and the International Red Cross. The Swiss economic miracle has continued since the Second World War with industries such as watch making, precision engineering and electrical generation becoming world leaders. Modern-day Switzerland has the highest nominal capital per head in the world and the second highest life expectancy. Transport systems by rail and road are world leaders and the country has an aura of order and cleanliness. The Swiss are justifiably proud of what they have achieved. European Union member countries surround Switzerland but it is not a member. The Swiss have, however, signed the Schengen accord, creating open borders with their neighbours, and are participants in the European Health Insurance Card system, allowing free emergency medical treatment to European visitors.

The neutrality conundrum

Switzerland has a policy of armed neutrality, with one of the highest levels of military expenditure per head in Europe. All Swiss men undertake military service with approximately 20 weeks' training upon reaching the age of 18, followed by annual exercises until 35. Conscripts keep their weapons and uniforms at home and on Saturday mornings armed men are often seen taking the train to annual camp. Prior to 1995 it was Swiss policy to sit out a nuclear war

Château de Chillon was a Savoyard castle captured by the Bernese (Stage 5A)

by retiring to nuclear bunkers in the hope of emerging unharmed when it was all over. All new buildings were built with nuclear shelters; these still exist with many used as underground garages or storerooms. Meanwhile the Swiss armed forces would retreat to fully equipped barracks in the fastness of the Alps, one of which is passed on Stage 4 at St Maurice. Airstrips were built in Alpine valleys with camouflaged hangars holding fighter aircraft ready to fly. Referenda in 1995 and 2003 scrapped this policy and reduced the armed forces from 400,000 to 200,000, although conscription remains.

Swiss languages
While it might appear that Switzerland, with four official languages – German (spoken by 72 per cent of the Swiss population), French (22 per cent), Italian (six per cent) and Romansh (under one per cent) – is a multilingual country, this is far from being true. Federal government business is conducted in German, French and Italian and school students are required to learn at least two languages. However, in most cantons, business is mono-lingual and it is sometimes difficult to find people willing to speak any Swiss language other than their own. Even Valais, where German is spoken in part of the canton and French in the rest, is not officially bilingual. The only places in Switzerland where bilingualism is legally prescribed are three towns that sit astride the isogloss (language border) including Sierre/Siders (Stage 2).

France
The Fifth French republic is the current manifestation of a great nation that developed out of Charlemagne's eighth-century Frankish kingdom and eventually spread its power throughout Europe and beyond.

Roman France
Before the arrival of the Romans in the first century BC, the part of France through which the Rhone flows was inhabited by Iron Age Celtic tribes such as the Gauls (central France) and Allobroges (Alpine France). The Romans involved local tribal leaders in government and control of the territory, and with improvements in the standard of living the conquered tribes soon became thoroughly Romanised. Roman colonial cities were established at places such as Lyon (Stage 10), Vienne (Stage 11) and Arles (Stage 19), with many other settlements all along the Rhone. During the fourth century AD, the Romans came under increasing pressure from Germanic tribes from the north and by AD401 had withdrawn their legions from the western Alps and Rhone valley.

The Franks and the foundation of France
After the Romans left there followed a period of tribal settlement. The Franks were a tribe that settled in northern France. From AD496, when Clovis I

Vienne's temple of Augustus and Livia is one of the best-preserved Roman buildings in France (Stage 11)

became their king and established a capital in Paris, the Frankish kingdom expanded by absorbing neighbouring states. After Charlemagne (a Frank, AD768–814) temporarily united much of western Europe, only for his Carolingian empire to be split in AD843, the Franks became the dominant regional force. Their kingdom, which became France, grew with expansion in all directions. To the southeast, the Dauphiné (the area between the Rhone and the Alps) was absorbed in 1349, Arles in 1378, Burgundy (north of Lyon) in 1477, Provence (the Mediterranean littoral) in 1481 and Franche-Comté (Jura) in

1678. Strong kings, including Louis XIV (1638–1715), ruled as absolute monarchs over a feudal kingdom with a rigid class system, the Ancien Régime. In many towns the church held as much power as the local nobility. Avignon was papal territory, ruled by a legate appointed by the Pope.

The French Revolution

The Ancien Régime French kingdom ended in a period of violent revolution (1789–1799). The monarchy was swept away and privileges enjoyed by the nobility and clergy were removed. Monasteries and religious institutions

17

were closed. In place of the monarchy a secular republic was established. The revolutionary mantra of 'liberté, égalité, fraternité' is still the motto of modern-day France. Chaos followed the revolution and a reign of terror resulted in an estimated 40,000 deaths, including King Louis XVI and his wife Marie Antoinette. A coup in 1799 led to military leader Napoléon Bonaparte taking control.

Napoléon Bonaparte

Despite ruling France for only 16 years, Napoléon (1769–1821) had a greater influence on the political and legal structures of Europe than any other person. He made peace with the Catholic church and allowed many exiled aristocrats to return, although with limited powers. In 1804 he declared himself Emperor of France and started a series of military campaigns that saw the French gain control of much of western and central Europe. Perhaps the longest lasting of the Napoleonic reforms was the 'Code Napoléon', a civil legal code that was adopted throughout the conquered territories and remains at the heart of the European legal system today. When he was defeated in 1815 by the combined forces of Britain and Prussia, he was replaced as head of state by a restoration of the monarchy under Louis XVIII, brother of Louis XVI.

Nineteenth-century France

Politically France went through a series of three monarchies, an empire headed by Napoléon III (Bonaparte's nephew) and two republics. Napoléon III's intervention in the reunification of

Cruise boats operate between Lyon (Stage 10) and Port-St Louis-du-Rhône (Stage 20)

Italy led to Savoy becoming part of France in 1860. During this period the French economy grew strongly, based upon coal, iron and steel and heavy engineering. A large overseas empire was created, mostly in Africa, second in size to the British Empire. Increasing conflict with Prussia and Germany led to defeat in the Franco-Prussian War (1870) and involvement in the First World War (1914–1918).

Twentieth-century France

Despite being on the winning side, the French economy was devastated by the war and the depression of the 1930s. Invasion by Germany in the Second World War (1939–1945) saw France partitioned temporarily, with all of southern France becoming part of Vichy, a nominally independent state that was in reality a puppet government controlled by the Germans. After the war, France was one of the original signatories to the Treaty of Rome (1957) which established the European Economic Community (EEC) and led to the European Union (EU). Economic growth was strong and the French economy prospered. Political dissent, particularly over colonial policy, led to a new constitution and the establishment of the fifth republic under Charles de Gaulle in 1958. Since then, withdrawal from overseas possessions has led to substantial immigration into metropolitan France from ex-colonies, creating the most ethnically diverse population in Europe. Large

cities like Lyon have suburbs with substantial immigrant populations. Since the 1970s, old heavy industry has almost completely disappeared and been replaced with high-tech industry and employment in the service sector.

Shipping on the river

Since Roman times the lower Rhone has been the main trade and communication route between the Mediterranean and central France, although strong currents and flooding caused by snow-melt in spring and low water levels in summer made navigation difficult. In the medieval period, freight was carried upriver in barge trains pulled by men and as many as 80 horses plodding along the towpath, while going downstream the barges flowed freely with the current. As the towpath was only used in one direction it is known as the *chemin de contre-halage*. Steam-powered boats replaced horses in the early 19th century. These were driven by two paddlewheels with some having a huge claw-wheel that gave extra power by gripping the riverbed. After the Second World War, steamboats were replaced by diesel powered barges. Tourist cruise boats operate on the lower river between Port-St Louis-du-Rhône and Lyon. Kilometre posts beside the navigable lower reaches of the river show distances downstream from the confluence of Rhone and Saône in Lyon.

The source of the Rhone is in the high Alps beside the Furkapass (Stage 1)

In 1933, the Compagnie Nationale du Rhône (CNR) was established to control the river. Work was halted by the Second World War but restarted in 1948. A series of 19 dams, 17 locks and a number of canal cuts have been constructed to improve navigation, generate electricity, control flooding and irrigate farmland. While the major works were completed in 1986, ongoing projects to open up the middle river above Lyon are continuing. The latest lock at Virignin (Stage 8) opened in 2012. Two dams have boat portage ramps (Brégnier-Cordon and Sault-Brénaz), although there are long-term plans to replace these with locks. When this infrastructure has been completed the river will be fully open to leisure craft as far as Seyssel, 461km from the Mediterranean.

Further upstream, the Seujet dam in Geneva (Stage 7) is the most important structure controlling both the level of Lake Geneva and the amount of water released into the Rhone. From 1894 the lake level was controlled by hand-operated sluices until being replaced by a hydroelectric dam in 1995.

THE RHONE CYCLE ROUTE

The 890km Rhone Cycle Route starts in the high Alps of central Switzerland, then heads west past Lake Geneva into France before turning south to reach the Mediterranean near Marseille. In Switzerland, it passes for 226km through the cantons of Valais, Vaud and Geneva, while the 664km in France mostly traverses the Auvergne-Rhône-Alpes region. Towards the end, the route follows the boundary between the regions of Occitanie and Provence-Alpes-Côte-d'Azur.

This route starts at the Rhone glacier viewpoint (Stage 1) beside the former Belvédère hotel, just west of the Furkapass summit. From here it plunges 900m downhill on the Furkapass to Oberwald then continues gently downhill through Goms, the pastoral valley of the infant Rhone, before descending a moraine to reach Brig in the upper part of Valais canton. Stages 2–3 continue through Valais, first passing the industrial town of Visp. Where the river drops over a second moraine, the route leaves the river, following a main road through Forêt de Finges pine forest. Between Sierre and Martigny the wide, straight valley is lined by vineyards and bound by snow-capped peaks. At Martigny, the river turns sharply north (Stage 4) between the Diablerets and Dents du Midi ranges, to reach the shore of Lake Geneva. There are alternative routes around the lake, with the ViaRhôna route passing to the south through the French towns of Évian and Thonon-les-Bains (Stages 5–6). The Swiss Rhone route R1 takes a 28km-longer and hillier route (Stages 5A and 6A), staying in Switzerland and going north of the lake via Montreux and Lausanne before re-joining the ViaRhôna in the cosmopolitan city of Geneva, which straddles the border between Switzerland and France.

Continuing through France, heading first southwest and then northwest, the route follows the winding river through the Rhone gorge cutting between the Jura and the Savoy Alps (Stages 7–9) with *balcons* (flat-topped limestone cliffs) on both sides. On Stage 10, population density increases as the route approaches Lyon, France's second largest city and gastronomic capital. From here it turns south (Stages 11–17) following a wide, relatively straight valley between the Alps to the east and Massif Central to the west, passing historic cities such as Vienne, Valence and Montélimar. This is an important transport route from northern Europe to the Mediterranean and the valley is followed by three railways (passenger, freight and high-speed), a national road (N7) and a motorway (A7), although these seldom impinge upon the cycle route. South of Vienne (Stage 12), vineyards line the valley and after Valence (Stage 15), which styles itself as the 'gateway to the south', the climate becomes mild enough for olives to survive the winter.

Beyond the papal capital of Avignon (Stage 18) the route reaches the flat lands of the Mediterranean littoral and the way of life, architecture and landscape become recognisably Provençale, immortalised by Vincent van Gogh in his paintings of the area around Arles (Stage 19). The final leg (Stage 20) takes the route through the sparsely inhabited flat lands of the

Rhone delta, known as the Camargue, to reach the Mediterranean 40km west of Marseille.

Physical geography

The course of the Rhone has been greatly influenced by geological events approximately 30 million years ago, when the Alps were pushed up by the collision of the African and European tectonic plates. As well as forming the Alps, this caused rippling of the landmass to the north, creating a ridge that forms the limestone mountains of the Jura and pushing up the older hard rocks of the Massif Central. Subsequent glaciation during a series of ice ages resulted in the Rhone cutting a series of deep U-shaped valleys through the high Alps (Stages 1–4). At the base of the glaciers a large lake formed (Lake Geneva, Stages 5–6). The outflow from this lake cut a winding gorge between the Jura mountains and Savoy Alps (Stages 7–10). At Lyon where the river reached the hard rock of the Massif Central, it was forced south through the wide and straight *sillon rhodanien* (Rhone furrow) all the way to the Mediterranean (Stages 11–18). As this valley was subject to frequent flooding the river developed a winding course through a marshy environment. For most of its length the river cuts down through soft limestone and carries large quantities of

sediment. Some of this sediment is deposited in Lake Geneva, which is slowly filling up although it will take many thousands of years to fill completely. The rest is carried down to the flat lands of the Mediterranean littoral (Stages 19–20), where the slow-flowing Rhone has deposited considerable quantities of sediment to form the Camargue delta.

The Rhone is the only one of Europe's great rivers that has an 'active' glacier as its main source, although this is now only 7km long compared with a length of 140km at the end of the last ice age 14,000 years ago. As the glacier retreated it left three terminal moraines (large piles of eroded rubble brought down by the glacier), which are crossed en route. The glacier is still retreating at about 10m per year and at this rate will disappear altogether in 700 years.

The Rhone is fed by a number of important tributaries including the Saône (draining the western slopes of the Jura) and the Isère, which rises in the Savoy Alps south of Mont Blanc.

Wildlife

While chamois and ibex can be found in the mountains near the source and a number of small mammals (including rabbits, hares, red squirrels, voles, water rats and weasels) may be seen scuttling across the track and deer glimpsed in forests, this is not a route for seeing wild animals. However, there are a few places where old bends of the river, abandoned since

Gardians (cowboys) from the Camargue gather in Arles for the annual bull running (Stage 19)

navigational improvements have made them redundant, have been turned into nature reserves. Of particular note is Printegarde nature reserve (Stage 15), home to many varieties of birds, animals and insects including black kites, storks, bee-eaters, European beaver and 40 varieties of dragonfly.

In the Camargue (Stage 20), two species of semi-feral animal can be found – black cattle and white horses. These animals are privately owned and tended by local *gardians* (cowboys) but are allowed to roam on the salt flats and marshes. The bulls are used to provide animals for local bull fights and for meat, while the horses are used as mounts for the gardians and for equestrian sports such as dressage and three-day eventing.

There is a wide range of interesting birdlife. White swans, geese and many varieties of ducks inhabit the river and its banks. Cruising above, raptors, particularly buzzards and kites, are frequently seen hunting small mammals, while flamingos can be found in the Camargue. Birds that live by fishing include cormorants, noticeable when perched on rocks with their wings spread out to dry,

23

Flamingos are common in the Camargue (Stage 20)

and grey herons, which can be seen standing in shallow water waiting to strike or stalking purposefully along the banks.

PREPARATION

When to go

With the exception of the first 14km of Stage 1, from the source beside the Furkapass to Oberwald, the route is generally cyclable from April to October. The Furkapass is blocked by snow in winter and is usually closed from November until May, exact dates varying from year to year depending upon snow levels. Indeed, snow can fall at any time of year, but is rare in July and August. The PostBus service over the pass, which can be used to reach the start of the route, runs only between mid June and mid October. As a result, unless you plan to cycle up to the source from Oberwald or Realp, the full ride can only be completed during summer and early autumn.

How long will it take?

The main route has been broken into 20 stages averaging 45km per stage. A fit cyclist, cycling an average of 74km per day should be able to complete the route in 12 days. A schedule for this timescale appears in the Twelve-day schedule. Travelling at a gentler pace of 60km per day and allowing time for sightseeing, cycling the Rhone to the Mediterranean would take a fortnight. There are many places to stay all along the route, making it is easy to tailor daily distances to your requirements.

What kind of cycle is suitable?

Most of the route is on asphalt cycle tracks or alongside quiet country roads. There are some stretches with gravel surfaces, particularly in Switzerland, but these are invariably well graded and pose few problems for touring cycles. However, cycling the exact route described in this guide is not recommended for narrow-tyred racing cycles. There are on-road alternatives which can be used to by-pass the rougher sections. The most suitable type of cycle is either a touring cycle or a hybrid (a lightweight but strong cross between a touring cycle and a mountain bike with at least 21 gears). There is no advantage in using a mountain bike. Front suspension is beneficial as it absorbs much of the vibration. Straight handlebars, with bar-ends enabling you to vary your position regularly, are recommended. Make sure your cycle is serviced and lubricated before you start, particularly the brakes, gears and chain.

As important as the cycle is your choice of tyres. Slick road tyres are not suitable and knobbly mountain bike tyres not necessary. What you need is something in-between with good tread and a slightly wider profile than you would use for everyday cycling at home. To reduce the chance of punctures, choose tyres with puncture resistant armouring, such as a Kevlar™ band.

GETTING THERE AND BACK

By rail
The start of the route near the summit of the Furkapass is not directly accessible by train. However, there are stations at Realp (east of the pass) and Oberwald (to the west) that are

A fully equipped cycle at Furka Belvédère (Stage 1)

PostBus services from Andermatt to Furka Belvédère carry up to six cycles (Prologue)

served by hourly year-round MGB (Matterhorn–Gotthard Bahn) narrow gauge trains between Andermatt and Brig. During the peak summer season (mid June to mid October) there is a PostBus service over the pass with two departures daily from Andermatt and three from Oberwald. These buses carry a limited number of cycles with reservations required before 1600 the previous day. Contact PostAuto Schweiz, Region Bern/Zentralalpen; +41 58 448 20 08; www.postauto.ch/bern. You can cycle up the pass, but this is a steep 900m climb on a main road from either Realp or Oberwald!

Andermatt can be reached by hourly SBB (Swiss railways) services

from Basle or Zürich, changing at Göschenen. Oberwald is accessed by hourly SBB services from Geneva and Lausanne, changing at Brig. If travelling from the UK, the most convenient approach is via Andermatt.

You can travel from the UK to Andermatt in a day via Paris, Strasbourg, Basle and Göschenen by leaving London early and having a cycle reservation on a lunchtime/early afternoon TGV train from Paris to Strasbourg. Eurostar trains from London St Pancras (not Ebbsfleet nor Ashford) to Paris Gare du Nord carry up to six cycles, two fully assembled plus four disassembled packed in special fibre glass cases which Eurostar supply. Passenger booking opens six months in advance at www.eurostar.com. A separate reservation is needed for your cycle which cannot be made online and must be obtained by phone (0344 822 5822). Costs vary between £30 and £55 depending on how far ahead you book, whether your bike is disassembled and if you want it to travel by the same train as you. Cycling UK members get a £5 discount. Bicycles need to be delivered to the EuroDespatch counter beside the coach drop-off point behind St Pancras station, at least one hour before departure. Allow 90 minutes if you need to disassemble your bike; despatch staff will provide the tools and can offer advice. EuroDespatch opens at 0700, so an early morning departure will require delivery the previous day. In Paris cycles are collected from the Geoparts luggage counter at Gare du Nord, reached by a path L of platform 3.

Frequent high-speed TGV Est trains run from Paris Gare de l'Est to Strasbourg but only a few have bicycle spaces. Details and bookings can be found on SNCF (French Railways) website: www.sncf-connect.com. Reservations (€10) are mandatory for cycles and must be purchased in advance with your passenger ticket. From Strasbourg you can connect to Basle by an hourly SNCF TER regional express train on which neither cycle ticket nor reservation are required. This should be booked separately as the SNCF booking system cannot handle journeys where one leg requires cycle reservations and another does not. From Basle, hourly Swiss Rail (SBB) trains take you on to Göschenen for Andermatt. A one-day cycle pass (CHF14) is needed on Swiss trains. Although most Swiss trains do not require cycle reservations, some IC inter-city trains on the Gotthard route used by Basel to Göschenen trains have mandatory reservations from 21 March to 31 October. Details at www.sbb.ch. Provision of cycle space on European trains changes frequently and up-to-date advice on travelling by train with a bicycle can be found on a website dedicated to worldwide rail travel, 'The man in seat 61' (www.seat61.com).

GARE DU NORD TO GARE DE L'EST

After arrival in Paris it is a short ride from Gare du Nord to Gare de l'Est. Go ahead opposite Gare du Nord's main exit along Bvd de Denain, a one-way street with contra-flow cycling permitted. At the end turn L (Bvd de Magenta) then fork L at second traffic lights (Rue du 8 Mai 1945) to reach Gare de l'Est (5min). Do not be tempted to use the route signposted for pedestrians. Although this is shorter, it involves a flight of stairs.

By air

Airports at Zürich (2hr 30min by train to Andermatt), Basle (3hr but you need to cycle from the airport to Basle station) or Geneva (4hr to Oberwald), all served by a variety of international airlines, can be used to access the Rhone source. Airlines have different requirements regarding how cycles are presented and some, but not all, make a charge, which you should pay when booking as it is usually greater at the airport. All require tyres partially deflated, handlebars turned and pedals removed (loosen pedals beforehand to make them easier to remove at the airport). Most will accept your cycle in a transparent polythene bike-bag, although some insist on use of a cardboard bike-box. These can be obtained from cycle shops, often for free, and may be purchased at some airports, including all terminals at Heathrow and Gatwick (Excess Baggage Company, www. left-baggage.co.uk).

By road

If you are lucky enough to have someone prepared to drive you to the start, Furkapass Belvédère is 2.5km west of Furkapass summit on Swiss national road 19 between Brig and Andermatt. With your own vehicle the most convenient place to leave it is Geneva, from where trains can be used to reach Oberwald on the outward journey, and which can be reached by train from Marseille on the return (see below). Geneva is between 800km

and 825km from the Channel ports depending upon route.

European Bike Express operates an overnight coach service with dedicated cycle trailer from northern England, picking up en route across England to the Mediterranean, with a drop-off point at Mâcon in eastern France. The journey time is between 13hr and 22hr depending on where the coach is joined. Details and booking through www.bike-express.co.uk. Trains link Mâcon with Geneva from where you can connect to Brig and Oberwald.

Intermediate access

There are international airports at Geneva (Stage 6) and Lyon (Stage 10). The airports at Sion (Stage 3) and Avignon (Stage 18) have very few international flights. Much of the route is closely followed by railway lines. Stations en route are listed in the text.

Getting home

The nearest station to Port-St Louis-du-Rhône is Fos-sur-Mer, 25km away by main road on the opposite side of the Golfe de Fos. The route to the station is described at the end of Stage 20. From here, regional local trains run to Miramas where you can connect with TER trains to Arles or Avignon Centre. Alternatively, local buses (route 1021) operated by Zou from Port-St Louis Douane (bus stop beside the blue lifting bridge) to Arles carry a limited number of cycles under the bus, with seven daily services Monday–Saturday, two on Sundays. Details from Zou +33 4 42 55 83 19 (www.zou.maregionsud.fr). From Arles, TER trains will take you to Avignon Centre and Lyon.

Only a few high-speed TGV Sud-Est trains from the South of France to Paris carry cycles. It may be necessary to use TER regional express trains and make the journey via a series of connections. From Arles or Avignon Centre it is possible to reach London in a day by leaving on an early morning TER service to Lyon, connecting there with another TER train to Paris and catching an early evening Eurostar to London. Journey time Arles–Paris by TER is between 8hr and 9hr. The direct afternoon Eurostar service from Marseille to London does not convey cycles. If you left a car in Switzerland, catch a TER train from Arles to Lyon and another from there to Geneva (every two hours). To fly home there are regular trains to Marseille Vitrolles airport, from where there are flights to many destinations.

European Bike Express (see above) can be used to get back to UK directly from the South of France. Nearest pick-up points are at Orange (25km north of Avignon) or Montpelier (70km west of Arles). Both can be reached by train from Arles.

NAVIGATION

Waymarking
The route follows two nationally designated cycle routes. In Switzerland Véloroute R1 (Rhone Route) is followed. This route is well established and waymarking is almost perfect in consistency. In France the route has been designated as ViaRhôna. This route has been in development since 2010 and by 2021, 95 per cent of waymarking was complete. Originally the route was designated as Véloroute V60, but this does not appear on waymarks where EuroVelo EV17 is used instead. While the planning of national cycle tracks is a regional government responsibility, implementation is delegated to départements (counties). Unfortunately provision of dedicated cycle tracks and waymarking varies between départements. In some parts of Haut Savoie (Stages 5/6), Rhône

Summary of cycle routes followed			
R1	Rhone Route	Stages 1–4, 5A–6A and 7	Switzerland
R46	Tour du Léman	Stage 6 and 5A–6A	Switzerland
VR	ViaRhôna	Stages 5–20	France
EV17	EuroVelo 17	Stages 1–20	Switzerland and France

Selected waymarkers along the route (clockwise from top left): Swiss R1; old style French ViaRhôna; provisional ViaRhôna; new French ViaRhôna with EV17 logo

(Stages 10/11) and Gard (Stage 19) the final route has not yet been designated and is either unwaymarked or indicated by yellow *provisoire* (provisional) waymarks. The route passing south of Lake Geneva (Stages 5–6) goes through both Swiss and French territory with waymarks for either R46 Tour de Léman and or ViaRhôna. In 2015 the whole route was accepted by the European Cyclists' Federation as EuroVelo route 17 and EV17 waymarks now appear on most signposts. In the introduction to each stage an indication is given of the predominant waymarks followed.

In France the route sometimes follows local roads. These are numbered as département roads (D roads). However, the numbering system can be confusing. Responsibility for roads has been devolved from national to local government and responsibility for many former *routes nationales* (N roads) has been transferred to local départements and renumbered as D roads. As départements have different systems of numbering, D road numbers often change when crossing département boundaries.

Maps

There are no published maps specifically covering the Rhone Cycle Route. Kümmerly & Frey publish a series of regional cycle maps that cover the Swiss part of the route (Stages 1–4).

Kümmerly & Frey (1:60,000)

- 22 Berner Oberland Ost, Goms
- 21 Oberwallis
- 20 Bas Valais, Sion
- 17 Genève

For the French section (Stages 5–20) the most suitable maps are regional road and leisure maps published by Michelin or IGN.

Michelin (1:150,000)

- 328 Ain, Haute-Savoie
- 333 Isère, Savoie
- 327 Loire, Rhône
- 332 Drôme, Vaucluse
- 340 Bouches-du-Rhône, Var

IGN (1:100,000)

- 143 Lons-le-Saunier, Genève
- 150 Lyon, Villefranche-sur-Saône
- 157 Grenoble, Montélimar
- 163 Avignon, Nîmes
- 171 Marseille, Avignon

Various online maps are available to download, at a scale of your choice. A strip map of the Swiss stages can be downloaded from www.veloland.ch, while the French stages can be found at www.viarhona.com. Particularly useful is Open Street Map (www.openstreetmap.org), which has a cycle route option showing the route in its entirety.

Guidebooks

Switzerland Mobility/WerdVerlag publish a guide for the Swiss Rhone route R1 available in French or German (not English), *La Suisse à Vélo/Veloland Schweiz volume 1 Route du Rhône/Rhone Route* (ISBN 9783859328518). Three French publishers, Chamina (ISBN 9782844664969), Editions Ouest (ISBN 9782737380792) and Le Routard (ISBN 9782017067665), all publish French language guides to the ViaRhôna. Esterbauer Bikeline publish separate guidebooks in German for the Swiss Rhone route R1 (ISBN 9783850009126) and ViaRhôna (ISBN 9783850009966).

Maps and guidebooks are available from leading bookshops including Stanfords, London and The Map Shop, Upton upon Severn. Relevant maps are widely available en route.

Hotels, guest houses and bed & breakfast

Along most of the route there is a wide variety of accommodation. The stage descriptions identify places known to have accommodation, but are by no means exhaustive. Hotels vary from expensive five-star properties to modest local establishments. Hotels usually offer a full meal service; guest houses do sometimes. *Chambres d'hôte* (bed and breakfasts) generally offer only breakfast. Tourist information offices, which are listed in Appendix B, will usually telephone on your behalf to check availability and make local reservations. After hours, some tourist offices display a sign outside showing local establishments with vacancies.

Booking ahead is seldom necessary, except in high season, although it is advisable to start looking for accommodation no later than 1600. Most properties are cycle friendly and will find you a secure overnight place for your pride and joy.

Prices for accommodation in France are similar to, or slightly cheaper than, prices in the UK. Switzerland is significantly more expensive.

Youth hostels

There are five official youth hostels on or near the route, three Swiss (Sion, Montreux, Lausanne) and two French (Lyon, Arles). To use a youth hostel (YH) you need to be a member of an association affiliated to Hostelling International (YHA in England, SYHA in Scotland). If you are not a member you will be required to join the local association. Rooms vary from single sex dormitories to family rooms with two to six beds. Unlike British hostels, most European hostels do not have self-catering facilities but do provide good value hot meals. Hostels get very busy, particularly during school holidays, and booking is advised through www.hihostels. com. The cities of Geneva and Avignon have privately owned backpacker hostels.

Gîtes d'étape are hostels and rural refuges mainly for walkers. They are mostly found in mountain areas, although there are ten on or near the ViaRhôna. Details of French gîtes d'étape can be found at www.gites-refuges.com. Do not confuse these with *Gîtes de France*, which are rural properties rented as weekly holiday homes. Hostels and gîtes d'étape are listed in Appendix C.

Camping

If you are prepared to carry camping equipment, this is the cheapest way of cycling the Rhone. The stage descriptions identify many official campsites but these are by no means exhaustive. Camping may be possible in other locations with the permission of local landowners.

FOOD AND DRINK

Where to eat

There are many places where cyclists can eat and drink, varying from snack bars, hot dog stands and local inns to Michelin-starred restaurants. Locations of many places to eat are listed in stage descriptions, but these are by no means exhaustive. English language menus are often available in big cities and tourist areas, but are less common in smaller towns and rural locations. Bars seldom serve food, although some offer snacks such as sandwiches, quiche Lorraine or croque-monsieur (a toasted ham and cheese sandwich). Tipping is not expected in Switzerland. In France, since 2008, tips are by law included in restaurant bills and must be passed on to the staff.

When to eat

Breakfast (German *Frühstück*, French *petit déjeuner*) is usually continental: breads, jam and a hot drink with the optional addition, particularly in Switzerland, of cold meats, cheese and a boiled egg. *Birchermüesli*, made from rolled oats, nuts and dried fruit, is the forerunner of commercially produced muesli.

Traditionally lunch (German *Mittagessen*, French *déjeuner*) was the main meal of the day, although this is slowly changing. Service usually ends by 1330 and if you arrive later you are unlikely to be served. Historically, French restaurants offered only a number of fixed price two-, three- and four-course meals at a number of price points. These often represent very good value, particularly for lunch if you want a three-course meal. Almost all restaurants nowadays also offer an à la carte menu and one course from this menu is usually enough at lunchtime if you plan an afternoon in the saddle. The most common lunchtime snacks everywhere are sandwiches, salads, quiche and croque-monsieur.

For dinner (German *Abendessen*, French *dîner*) a wide variety of cuisine is available. Much of what is available is pan-European and will be easily recognisable. There are, however, national and regional dishes you may wish to try.

What to eat

As francophone Switzerland is mainly an agricultural area, regional dishes tend to make use of local produce, particularly vegetables and dairy

Fondue made with Swiss cheese

FROM ESCOFFIER TO NOUVELLE CUISINE

France is widely regarded as a place where the preparation and presentation of food is central to the country's culture. Modern-day French cuisine was first codified by Georges Auguste Escoffier in *Le Guide Culinaire* (1903). Central to Escoffier's method was the use of light sauces made from stocks and broths to enhance the flavour of the dish in place of heavy sauces that had previously been used to mask the taste of bad meat. French cooking was further refined in the 1960s with the arrival of nouvelle cuisine which sought to simplify techniques, lessen cooking time and preserve natural flavours by changing cooking methods. This was pioneered at La Pyramide in Vienne (Stage 11) and taken up enthusiastically by the late Paul Bocuse who operated a number of restaurants in Lyon (Stage 10), often described as the world capital of gastronomy.

products. Varieties of cheese include Emmental, Gruyère and Vacherin. The high Alpine valleys provide good conditions for drying hams and bacon. *Rösti* is finely grated potato, fried and often served with bacon and cheese while *raclette* is made from grilled slices of cheese drizzled over potatoes and gherkins. The most famous cheese dish is fondue, melted cheese flavoured with wine and used as a dipping sauce. *Papet Vaudois* is a dish of leeks and potatoes usually served with sausage. For meat, veal sourced from male calves produced by dairy cattle herds, is popular. *Geschnetzeltes* (*veau a la mode Zurich* in French) are thin slices of veal in cream and mushroom sauce. The most common fish are trout from mountain streams and zander (often referred to as pike-perch) found in Swiss lakes. As Swiss cooking uses a lot of salt, it is advisable to taste your food before

adding any more. Switzerland is rightly famous for its chocolate and the headquarters of Nestlé, the inventors of milk chocolate bars, are passed in Vevey (Stage 5).

French Savoyard cuisine is similar to that of neighbouring regions in Switzerland and many of the same dishes can be found. A local speciality is *tartiflette*, a casserole of potatoes, bacon lardons and onions covered with melted Reblochon cheese.

Local specialities in Lyon include *mâchons*, morning snacks made from charcuterie accompanied by Beaujolais red wine and formerly eaten by silk workers. Other dishes include *rosette de Lyon* (cured pork sausage served in chunky slices), *salade lyonnaise* (lettuce, bacon and poached egg), *cervelle de canut* (cheese spread made with herbs, shallots, olive oil and vinegar), *pommes de terre lyonnaise* (potatoes sautéed with onions and parsley) and *quenelles de brochet* (creamed pike in an egg-based mousse).

Provençale cooking in southern France makes use of local herbs, olives, olive oil and vegetables including tomatoes, peppers, aubergines and garlic. A traditional Provençale dish is *ratatouille*, a vegetable stew of tomatoes, peppers, onions, aubergines and courgettes. *Daube Provençale* is beef and vegetables stewed in red wine. In the Camargue, local black bulls are sometimes used for the meat in daube. Mediterranean fish are widely used, a typical dish being *bouillabaisse* fish stew with tomatoes, onions and herbs.

Rice is grown in the Camargue, the most northerly place in Europe it can be cultivated.

What to drink

The Rhone flows through some of the greatest wine-producing regions of both Switzerland and France. In Switzerland the vineyards of Valais (Stage 3), Chablais (Stage 4) and Lavaux (Stage 5A) both in Vaud, and La Côte (Stage 6) near Geneva produce mostly Fendant dry white wine from chasselas grapes and Dôle soft red wine from pinot noir and gamay grapes. Swiss wine is one of Europe's best-kept secrets as the Swiss consume

Local wine bottles outside a wine merchant in l'Hermitage (Stage 13)

almost all the production and export very little. Wine by the glass in restaurants is usually priced by the decilitre (1dl = 100ml) and is served in 1dl, 2dl or 5dl carafes. The nearest equivalent to a UK 175ml standard glass is 2dl.

The French regard themselves as the world's premier quality wine-producing nation and some of the highest-quality wines are made in the Rhone valley, particularly at l'Hermitage (Stage 13) and Châteauneuf-du-Pape (Stage 18), both producing full-bodied red wine. Other areas producing AC (*appellation contrôlée*) quality wines include Seyssel dry white and sparkling wine in Savoy (Stage 7), Côte-Rôtie red wine and Condrieu white wine from viognier grapes (Stage 12) and Tavel and Lirac rosé wine (Stage 19). The greatest quantity of wine, however, comes from 150 AC communes known collectively as the Côtes du Rhône that spread throughout the lower valley from Vienne to Avignon (Stages 12–18) and from an even greater number of vineyards in Gard (Stages 18–19) producing VDQS and Vin de Pays wine (less rigorous quality standards, but nevertheless very drinkable and considerably cheaper) mostly from carignan and grenache grapes. Listel, the largest producer in France, produces high-quality wines from vineyards on the sands of the Petit Camargue, fertilised by bringing mountain sheep down from the hills to graze the vineyards in winter. They are particularly known for Gris de Gris, white wine made from red grape varieties.

Although western Switzerland and southern France are predominantly wine drinking areas, beer consumption is increasing. Main varieties are blonde (light-coloured lager) and blanche (cloudy, slightly sweet tasting beer made from wheat). Pan-European breweries, such as Kronenbourg and Heineken, produce most of the beer. However, there are a growing number of *brasserie artisanal* (craft breweries) brewing distinct local beers.

All the usual soft drinks (colas, lemonade, fruit juices, mineral waters) are widely available. Local specialities include Rivella, a Swiss drink sweetened with lactose (milk sugars) and available in a number of varieties. The spring from which Evian water (one of the world's biggest mineral water brands) is sourced is passed on Stage 5.

AMENITIES AND SERVICES

Grocery shops

All cities, towns and larger villages passed through have grocery stores, often supermarkets, and most have pharmacies. Even small villages have *boulangeries* (bakers), which open early and produce fresh bread throughout the day. Shop opening hours vary and in southern France many shops close in the afternoon between 1300 and 1600.

Cycle shops

The route is well provided with cycle shops, most with repair facilities. Locations are listed in the stage descriptions, although this is not exhaustive. Many cycle shops will adjust brakes and gears, or lubricate your chain, while you wait, often not seeking reimbursement for minor repairs. Touring cyclists should not abuse this generosity and should always offer to pay, even if this is refused.

Currency and banks

France switched from the French franc to the €uro in 2002. In Switzerland the Swiss franc (CHF) is used. This is a very strong currency, which has appreciated noticeably against the €uro in recent years, making prices in Switzerland relatively high. In places near the Franco/Swiss border it is usually considerably cheaper to eat, drink and sleep in France rather than Switzerland. Almost every town has a bank and most have ATM machines that enable you to make transactions in English. Contact your bank to activate your bankcard for use in Europe.

Telephone and internet

The whole route has mobile phone (German: *handy*) coverage. Contact your network provider to ensure your phone is enabled for foreign use with the most economic price package. International dialling codes from UK (+44) are:

- +41 Switzerland
- +33 France

    Most hotels, guest houses and hostels make internet access freely available to guests.

Electricity

Voltage is 220v, 50HzAC. Plugs are standard European two-pin round, with a third 'earth' pin incorporated in the socket.

Clothing and personal items

Even though the route is predominantly downhill, weight should be kept to a minimum. You will need clothes for cycling (shoes, socks, shorts/trousers, shirt, fleece, waterproofs) and clothes for evenings and days-off. The best maxim is two of each, 'one to wear, one to wash'. Time of year makes a difference as you need more and warmer clothing in April/May and September/October. All of this clothing should be easy to wash en route, and a small tube or bottle of travel wash is useful. A sun hat and sun glasses are essential, while gloves and a woolly hat are advisable except in high summer.

    In addition to your usual toiletries you will need sun cream and lip salve. You should take a simple first-aid kit. If staying in hostels you will need a towel and torch (your cycle light should suffice).

The Goms valley between Mühlebach and Ernen with Finsteraarhorn (4274m) in the distance (Stage 1)

Cycle equipment

Everything you take needs to be carried on your cycle. If overnighting in accommodation, a pair of rear panniers should be sufficient to carry all your clothing and equipment, but if camping, you may also need front panniers. Panniers should be 100 per cent watertight. If in doubt, pack everything inside a strong polythene lining bag. Rubble bags, obtainable from builders' merchants, are ideal for this purpose. A bar-bag is a useful way of carrying items you need to access quickly such as maps, sunglasses, camera, spare tubes, puncture-kit and tools. A transparent map case attached to the top of your bar-bag is

an ideal way of displaying maps and guidebook.

Your cycle should be fitted with mudguards and bell, and be capable of carrying water bottles, pump and lights. Many cyclists fit an odometer to measure distances. A basic tool-kit should consist of puncture repair kit, spanners, Allen keys, adjustable spanner, screwdriver, spoke key and chain repair tool. The only essential spares are two spare tubes. On a long cycle ride, sometimes on dusty tracks, your chain will need regular lubrication and you should either carry a can of spray-lube or make regular visits to cycle shops. A good strong lock is advisable.

SAFETY AND EMERGENCIES

Weather

The first half of the route is in the continental climate zone, typified by warm dry summers interspersed with short periods of heavy rain and cold winters. Below Lyon the route enters the Mediterranean zone with hot dry summers and mild damp autumns and winters. The greatest rainfall is in autumn and often occurs in heavy downpours. The beginning of Stage 1 is exposed to mountain weather with heavy winter snowfall, which in some years can remain on the ground until June.

The Rhone valley south of Lyon and the Mediterranean coast are subject to the Mistral, a strong cold but dry wind that blows from the north to the south down the valley. It is most common in winter and spring, but can occur at any time of year. Mistral winds often exceed 40kph during the day, but die down at night. As the route in this guide runs north to south, if the Mistral is blowing it will be behind you!

Road safety

Throughout the route, cycling is on the right side of the road. If you have never cycled on the right you will quickly adapt, but roundabouts may prove challenging. You are most prone to mistakes when setting off each morning. Both Switzerland and France are very cycle-friendly countries. Drivers will normally give you plenty of space when overtaking and often wait behind patiently until space to pass is available.

Average temperatures (max/min°C)

	Apr	May	Jun	Jul	Aug	Sep	Oct
Andermatt	2/-1	7/3	10/5	12/8	12/7	9/5	5/2
Geneva	15/5	20/9	24/12	27/14	26/14	21/11	15/7
Lyon	16/7	21/11	25/14	28/17	27/16	23/13	17/9
Avignon	19/8	23/12	27/15	31/18	30/18	25/14	20/11

Average rainfall (mm/rainy days)

	Apr	May	Jun	Jul	Aug	Sep	Oct
Andermatt	135/14	128/14	119/14	108/12	128/13	109/10	120/10
Geneva	72/10	84/11	92/10	79/8	82/9	101/8	105/8
Lyon	75/9	91/11	76/8	64/7	62/7	88/8	99/10
Avignon	66/11	65/12	38/9	37/6	42/8	102/8	93/10

Much of the route is on dedicated cycle paths, although care is necessary as these are sometimes shared with pedestrians. Use your bell, politely, when approaching pedestrians from behind. Where you are required to cycle on the road there is usually a dedicated cycle lane. Some city and town centres have pedestrian-only zones. These restrictions are often only loosely enforced and you may find local residents cycling within them; indeed many zones have signs allowing cycling. Many one-way streets have signs permitting contra-flow cycling.

Neither Switzerland nor France require compulsory wearing of cycle helmets, although their use is recommended. Modern lightweight helmets with improved ventilation are more comfortable to wear.

In Switzerland, cycling after drinking alcohol has the same 50mg/100ml limit as drink-driving (English drink-driving limit is 80mg/100ml). If you cycle after drinking and are caught, you could be fined and banned from driving and cycling in Switzerland.

Emergencies

In the unlikely event of an accident, the standardised EU and Swiss emergency phone number is 112. The entire route has mobile phone coverage. Prior to Jan 2021, an EHIC card issued by your home country provided free access to medical care in state-run establishments in both France and Switzerland. When the UK left the EU, two changes occurred.

Firstly a GHIC card replaced the EHIC card, although existing EHIC cards remain valid for up to five years until they expire. Secondly UK-issued cards now only cover EU countries and neither is valid in Switzerland. In France you may have to pay up-front and claim costs back through the Caisse Primaire d'Assurance-Maladie (CPAM) so make sure you keep all the paperwork. Helicopter rescue, ambulance use and repatriation are not covered and you will have to pay directly and claim costs back through travel insurance.

Theft

In general the route is safe and the risk of theft very low, particularly in Switzerland. However, you should always lock your cycle and watch your belongings, especially in cities.

Insurance

Since UK-issued EHIC/GHIC cards no longer cover Switzerland, travel insurance with health cover is essential. Such policies usually cover you when cycle touring but they do not normally cover damage to, or theft of, your bicycle. If you have a household contents policy, this may cover cycle theft, but limits may be less than the real cost of your cycle. Cycling UK (formerly the Cyclists' Touring Club), www.cyclinguk.org, offer a policy tailored for your needs when cycle touring.

If you live in Switzerland and own a bicycle, you need to purchase an annual vélo vignette, a registration

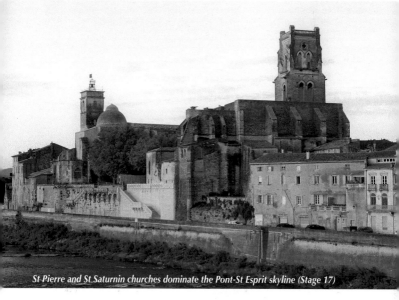

St Pierre and St Saturnin churches dominate the Pont-St Esprit skyline (Stage 17)

sticker that includes compulsory third-party insurance. However, this is not a requirement for short-term visitors.

ABOUT THIS GUIDE

Text and maps

There are 20 stages, each covered by separate maps drawn to a scale of 1:100,000. Signposting and waymarking are generally good and by combining these with the maps and stage descriptions, it is possible to cycle the route without the expense or weight of carrying a large number of other maps. Beware, however, as the route described here does not

always exactly follow the waymarked route. Gradient profiles are provided for stages 1–7 where there are significant changes of altitude. Other stages are level or nearly level.

Places that appear on the maps are shown **bold** in the text. The abbreviation 'sp' in the text indicates a signpost. Distances shown are cumulative within each stage. For each city/town/village passed an indication is given of facilities available (accommodation, refreshments, YH/gîte, camping, tourist office, cycle shop, station) when the guide was written, and this information is summarised in Appendix A. This list is neither exhaustive nor does it guarantee that establishments are still in business. No attempt has been made to list all such facilities as this would require another book the same size as this one. For full listing of accommodation, contact local tourist offices. Such listings are usually available online. Tourist offices along the route are listed in Appendix B.

While route descriptions were accurate at the time of writing, things do change. Temporary diversions may be necessary to circumnavigate improvement works and permanent diversions to incorporate new sections of cycle track. This is particularly the case in France where parts of the route are classified as 'provisional' as work to provide a separate cycle route is planned but has not yet been implemented. Where construction is in progress you may find signs showing recommended diversions, although these are likely to be in French only.

Some alternative routes exist. Where these offer a reasonable variant, usually because they are either shorter or offer a better surface, they are described in the text and shown in blue on the maps.

GPX tracks

GPX tracks for the routes in this guidebook are available to download free at www.cicerone.co.uk/1082/GPX. If you have not bought the book through the Cicerone website, or have bought the book without opening an account, please register your purchase in your Cicerone library to access GPX and update information.

A GPS device is an excellent aid to navigation, but you should also carry a map and compass and know how to use them. GPX files are provided in good faith, but in view of the profusion of formats and devices, neither the author nor the publisher accepts responsibility for their use. We provide files in a single standard GPX format that works on most devices and systems, but you may need to convert files to your preferred format using a GPX converter such as gpsvisualizer.com or one of the many other apps and online converters available.

Language

Apart from Stages 1–2, where Swiss German is spoken, the route is through the francophone (French-speaking) part of Switzerland and France. Throughout this guide the English spelling 'Rhone' is used. In Swiss German the river is known as the Rotten, in French as the Rhône. Place names and street names are given in appropriate local languages, German for Stages 1–2 and French for the rest of the route. Exceptions are made for Lake Geneva (Lac Léman in French), Geneva (Genève) and Savoy (Savoie); although compound proper nouns (Anthy-sur-Léman, Côte du Rhône, Haute-Savoie, etc) appear in French. See Appendix E for a list of useful French and German words.

THE ROUTE

The infant Rhone makes its way from the Rhone glacier towards Gletsch (Stage 1)

PROLOGUE
Andermatt or Oberwald to Furkapass

Start	Realp station (1538m) or Oberwald station (1366m)
Finish	Furkapass, Belvédère (2275m)
Distance	15km (Realp), 14km (Oberwald)
Ascent	891m (Realp), 909m (Oberwald)
Descent	154m (Realp), 0m (Oberwald)
Waymarking	Rhone route R1

The nearest stations to the Rhone source are Realp, east of the Furkapass, and Oberwald, west of it. There is nothing to choose between them as from Realp it is a 15km ride with nearly 900m of ascent, while from Oberwald it is a 14km ride with a similar ascent. If you ascend from Oberwald, you will be retracing this route for the first 14km of Stage 1. If you are cycling the route between mid June and mid October you can avoid the climb by using a cycle-carrying PostBus service which crosses the pass en route between Andermatt and Oberwald, alighting at Furka Belvédère. If the pass is closed by snow (which can happen at any time of year), you will have to start your journey to the Mediterranean from Oberwald station. Trains run all year between Realp and Oberwald through the Furka base tunnel.

From Realp station

From **Realp** station (1538m) (accommodation, refreshments, station), go straight ahead away from the station along Bahnhofstrasse. After 75m, turn L onto main road (Furkastrasse, route 19) and continue out of village, starting to climb immediately. ◄ Pass station and workshops of Furka–Oberwald steam cogwheel railway L and start ascending Furkapass steeply round series of nine hairpin bends. Pass Galenstock (5.5km, 2000m) and continue climbing across bare hillside above treeline past Tiefenbach. After two more hairpins pass Furkablick to reach car park and viewpoint at **Furkapass** summit

Furkastrasse is a main road with no cycle lane.

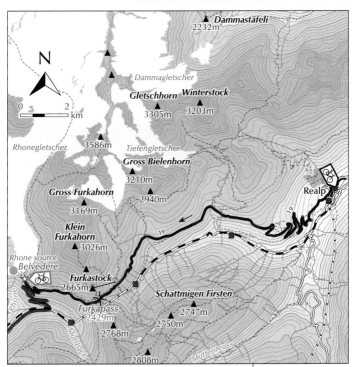

(12km, 2429m). ▶ Road now starts descending through another series of hairpin bends and reaches **Furka Belvédère** complex on apex of third bend (15km, 2275m) (refreshments).

From Oberwald station

From the main entrance to **Oberwald** station (1366m), turn R to join main road (Furkastrasse, route 19). Follow this through Oberwald village (accommodation, refreshments, tourist office, cycle shop, station) and start ascending through woodland round four hairpin bends, passing St Niklaus chapel on first bend and Rhonequelle hotel (accommodation, refreshments) on fourth. Pass

At Furkapass summit you cross the watershed between rivers flowing via the Rhine to the North Sea and the Rhone flowing south to the Mediterranean.

For map see Stage 1.

45

through short tunnel and round four more bends to reach **Gletsch** (6.5km, 1762m) (accommodation, refreshments, tourist office, station). Pass station and bear R past junction with Grimselpass road. ◄ Continue ascending through forest round four more hairpins and after emerging above treeline reach final set of bends with **Furka Belvédère** complex on apex of sixth bend (14km, 2275m) (refreshments).

Gletsch station is served by Furka–Oberwald cogwheel steam trains that operate only in summer.

The **Rhone source** is a small lake below the head of the glacier, which can be seen beyond the Belvédère viewpoint. A footpath leads 400m from the Belvédère viewpoint across glacially scoured bare rock to the outflow from this lake.

The **Rhone glacier** is a 7km tongue of ice running down the south side of Dammastock. The ice-cap on top of this mountain also feeds glaciers running north towards the Sustenpass and east towards Göschenen. Like all glaciers in the Alps it is steadily retreating. Pictures from the 1870s show the glacier reaching all the way down the valley to Gletsch. Since then it has retreated 1.4km to its current outflow below the Furka Belvédère. An ice grotto for visitors and tunnels for scientific research have been cut into the ice wall and are renewed annually. White insulating blankets have been placed over the end of the glacier above the ice grotto in an attempt to slow icemelt. They seem to be effective as the ice is clearly thicker at this point.

The Rhone source is fed by a glacier running down from Dammastock

47

STAGE 1
Furkapass to Brig

Start	Furkapass, Belvédère (2275m)
Finish	Brig (Naters), Rottubrigga bridge (671m)
Distance	55.5km; off-road via Binntal 62.5km
Ascent	197m; via Binntal 379m
Descent	1801m; via Binntal 1983m
Waymarking	Rhone route R1 (goes via Binntal)

The first stage begins by descending the Furkapass on the main road to Oberwald, then continues on quiet country lanes and cycle tracks through the flower-filled meadows of Goms, the wide high-level valley of the infant Rhone. After Ernen the waymarked route uses rough tracks, with a very steep descent and ascent through Binntal suitable for experienced off-roaders only. The route described here avoids this by following the main road.

From **Furka Belvédère**, follow main road (Furkastrasse, route 19) downhill round five hairpin bends. Enter forest and continue round four more bends to reach **Gletsch** (7.5km, 1762m) (accommodation, refreshments, tourist office, station).

The tiny settlement of **Gletsch**, which means 'glacier' in local dialect, is an important Alpine road junction between routes over the Furka and Grimsel passes. In the 19th century the Rhone glacier reached all the way down to Gletsch and the Glacier du Rhône hotel was built to house tourists drawn to see the ice. As many of these tourists were English, a small Anglican chapel was built which still holds fortnightly services.

Pass Grimselpass road R and Gletsch station L, then continue descending round four more bends and pass

Descending the Furkapass below the rock wall of the retreating Rhone glacier

49

Beware, the road surface in the tunnel is cobbles.

through short tunnel. ◀ After passing Rhonequelle hotel L (accommodation, refreshments), another series of four bends takes you down through woods to beginning of **Oberwald** (14km, 1366m) (accommodation, refreshments, tourist office, cycle shop, station).

> **Oberwald** (pop 230) is a small winter sport and agricultural settlement at the point where the Furka–Oberwald railway branches off the Matterhorn–Gotthard Bahn (MGB) main line. Originally all trains ran via the old Furka tunnel at 2163m. Only a summer seasonal service was operated as every winter a narrow bridge had to be dismantled to avoid damage from heavy snowfall. When a new line was opened through the Furka base tunnel (1982), with a year-round service, the old line was abandoned. In 1992, a preservation society was formed with the objective of reopening the line. After many years of work the line was fully reopened in 2010, using original steam cogwheel locomotives which had been sold to Vietnam when the line was electrified and then repatriated and renovated to operate the line.

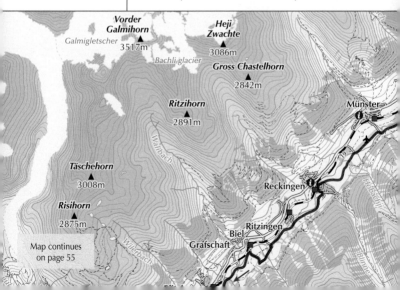

Map continues on page 55

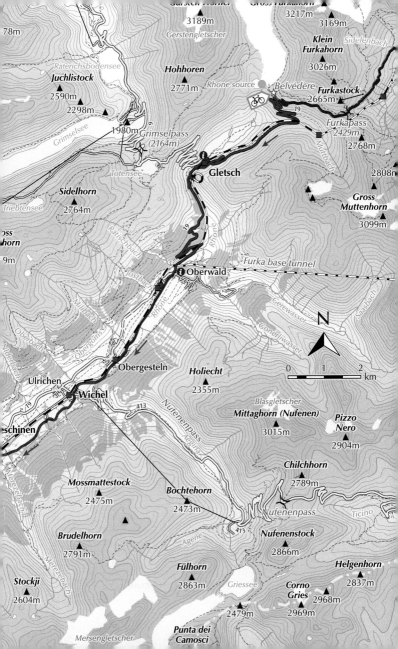

Trains between Oberwald and Realp run in summer only, with one trip on weekdays and up to three at weekends.

At first road junction in village, where main road bears R, fork L ahead (Rottenstrasse) beside the fast-flowing Rhone. Pass railway station R and continue between river L and railway R to **Obergesteln** (16.5km, 1355m) (accommodation, refreshments, station).

The village of **Obergesteln** is unusual for the area in that many of the buildings are constructed from stone rather than wood. This is the result of two 19th-century fires that destroyed the village. After the second fire (1868) the cantonal authorities dictated that buildings be rebuilt in stone.

The runway is on the opposite side of the river and railway, requiring planes to cross a bridge and railway level crossing to take off.

Turn L across Rhone, and R to continue along opposite bank. After 150m fork R onto gravel cycle track following river. At Ulrichen bridge (18km, 1350m), dog-leg L and R across road through **Wichel** (accommodation, refreshments, camping, station). Cross small stream and bear R, passing campsite R. Cycle track bears away from river passing camouflaged hangars and bunkers of disused military airfield. ◄ After last hangar, fork R and follow track winding through fields with wooded hillside rising L before returning to river at **Geschinen** bridge (station). Turn L along riverbank (do not cross river) on unsurfaced cycle track. Turn R on quiet road and continue over Rhone on **Münster** bridge (22.5km, 1335m). ◄

To visit Münster (accommodation, refreshments, tourist office, station) continue ahead for 500m after crossing the river.

Münster (pop 500), the principal community of upper Goms, has many vernacular wooden buildings, some from the 15th century. Typical Goms houses, with their bronzed appearance, are constructed of larch that has darkened with centuries of exposure to strong sunlight. Many stand on saddle stones to prevent rodent ingress. The white-painted St Maria parish church has an altar regarded as the second most beautiful in

Switzerland (after Chur cathedral), together with ancient choir stalls and a fine ceiling.

After crossing bridge, continue for 50m then turn L on perimeter road beside another airfield runway passing series of camouflaged hangars L. At end of runway, where gliders are sometimes parked, turn L on bridge across Rhone. Bear R and continue winding through fields to **Reckingen** (25km, 1317m) (accommodation, refreshments, camping, tourist office, station). Turn L beside river (do not cross covered bridge) then bear L and turn R on bridge over small stream. Pass through campsite and leave village on gravel track beside river. Where track turns sharply R around waterworks, bear L on unsurfaced track through field towards two barns. Follow this track back to riverside and continue through woods climbing very steeply over a ridge, then

Wooden houses in Goms turned black by centuries of exposure to strong sunlight

Oberaletschgletscher   Mittelaletschgletscher

Vord Geisshorn ▲
3583m

Geisshorn ▲
3740m

Rotstock ▲
3699m

Gross Fusshorn ▲
3627m

Sparrhorn ▲
3021m

Aletsch glacier

Strahlhorn ▲
3026m

Märjelen-Stausee

Eggishorn ▲
2926m

Elselicka ▲
2722m

Fiescheralp

Bettmersee

Bettmeralp

Martisberg

Stausee
Gibidum

Riederhorn ▲
2230m

Riederalp

Goppisberg

Greich

Betten

19

Grengiols

Belalp

Aletschwald

Breiten

ℹ Filet

Bister

Blatten

Sommerseili   Ried

Mörel

Tunetschalp

Chieleibach

Massa

Chriesihorn ▲

Bättlihorn ▲
2992m

Geimen

Bitsch

Eiste

Chleine Huwetz ▲
2918m

19

Termen

Naters

Grau
Horl

🚲

ℹ **BRIG**

Fülhorn ▲
2738m

Seewjihorn ▲
2733m

gisch

Glis

Ried-
Brig

Rosswald

Schiessbach

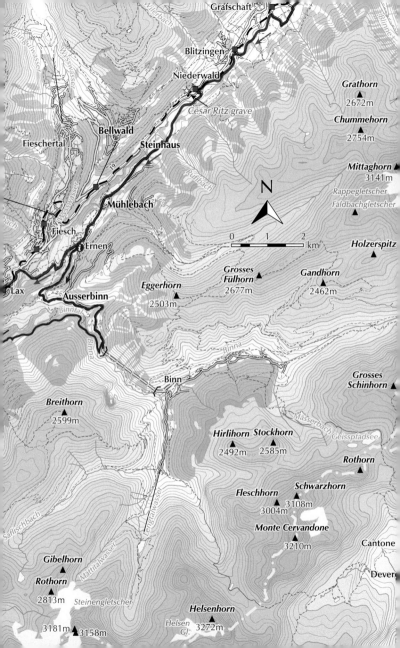

Grafschaft

Blitzingen

Niederwald

César Ritz grave

Bellwald

Fiechertal

Steinhaus

Grathorn
▲
2672m

Chummehorn
▲
2754m

Mittaghorn ▲
3141m

Rappegletscher

Fäldbachgletscher
▲

Mühlebach

N

0   1   2
━━━━━━━━━ km

Holzerspitz
▲

Fiesch

Ernen

Eggerhorn
▲
2503m

Grosses
Fülhorn
2677m ▲

Gandhorn
▲
2462m

Lax

Ausserbinn

Binna

Binn

Binntal

Grosses
Schinhorn
▲

Masserbach

Geisspfadsee

Breithorn
▲
2599m

Hirlihorn
▲
2492m

Stockhorn
▲
2585m

Rothorn
▲

Säflischbach

Fleschhorn
▲
3004m

Schwarzhorn
▲
3108m

Mättital-wasser

Fengstalwasser

Monte Cervandone
▲
3210m

Cantone

Dever

Gibelhorn
▲

Rothorn
▲
2813m

Steinengletscher

3181m ▲▲ 3158m

Helsenhorn
▲
3272m

Helsen
Gl.

descend to **Ritzingen** bridge (camping, station). Turn L (do not cross river) and follow road curving R and fork L through campsite and on into open woodland climbing less steeply over another ridge. At end of campsite fork R and follow road descending round sharp R bend to river at **Biel** bridge (station).

Turn L along riverbank (do not cross bridge) and follow track through forest. Pass **Grafschaft** bridge R and continue on winding gravel track more or less parallel with river to **Blitzingen** bridge (30.5km, 1257m) (accommodation, refreshments, station). Continue past bridge on riverside track with wooded hillside rising L and cross river at next bridge. Ascend from river to reach railway and fork L beside railway to reach T-junction at level crossing by **Niederwald** station (32km, 1242m) (refreshments, station).

CÉSAR RITZ

Niederwald was the birthplace of international hotelier César Ritz (1850–1918). He was born into a peasant family and his catering career started as an apprentice sommelier in Brig. Moving jobs regularly, he left Switzerland (1867) to ply his trade in Paris. In 1873 he moved to Nice as restaurant manager of the Grand Hotel and moved up to manage Grand Hotels in Lucerne and Monte Carlo. In 1888 he teamed up with leading chef Auguste Escoffier to open a restaurant in Baden-Baden and the two were then invited to London to manage the Savoy hotel. Mixing with the rich and famous, he was described by the Prince of Wales as 'the king of hoteliers and hotelier to kings'. He left under a cloud (1898) after allegations of misappropriating £3400 of wines and spirits. He and Escoffier soon opened their own hotel in Paris (The Ritz) and went on to open Ritz hotels in London (1906), Madrid (1910) and other cities. When he died he was initially buried in Père Lachaise cemetery (Paris) but was reinterred in Niederwald in 1961.

Turn L away from railway then L again to reach river. Cross river by Niederwald bridge and fork R along riverbank track. Cross small stream and continue on winding track that climbs through fields away from Rhone. Join country road and cross river Rufibach into **Steinhaus**.

Continue on road, passing through short tunnel, to reach **Mühlebach** (accommodation, refreshments). ▶ Pass through lower part of village (Neue Mühlebachstrasse) and continue on road (Hengert) into **Ernen** (38km, 1200m) (accommodation, refreshments, tourist office).

There is a sharp bend in the tunnel.

> **Ernen** (pop 520), which sits on a moraine terrace above the Rhone valley, is one of the most attractive villages in Valais with houses dating from the 15th to 18th centuries. The Tellenhaus (1578) is decorated with the earliest known depiction of the William Tell legend. Ernen calls itself 'musikdorf' (village of music) and is the venue for a music festival every summer. This started in 1974 when György Sebök, a Hungarian pianist who had settled in Ernen, started giving annual masterclasses for pianists and chamber musicians. In 1987 the masterclasses were enhanced with a series of concerts held in the sumptuously decorated church, which has a renowned organ and excellent acoustics. Nowadays, in addition to masterclasses, the eight-week festival (July–August) includes piano recitals; chamber, baroque, jazz and orchestral concerts; and writing workshops.

Off-road route via Binntal
Fork L by Ernen village square to continue on Binntalstrasse. This curves S, ascending gently through forest with Binntal valley below R, to reach **Ausserbinn** (3.5km, 1286m) (accommodation, refreshments). Continue past hamlet for 2km and, 200m before road enters long tunnel, turn sharply R onto track that descends very steeply on rough track round two zigzag bends into Binntal. Cross bridge over river Binna and ascend on gravel track winding through forest on other side of valley. After passing chapel, track descends through series of alpine meadows to reach a road head. Continue on road, with view of confluence of Binna and Rhone below R, through small hamlet of Bächerhyschere (accommodation, refreshments) and over bridge on hairpin bend to reach Oberdorf above village

of **Grengiols** (11.5km, 1029m) (accommodation, refreshments, station in valley below).

> **Grengiols** (pop 430) is home to a unique wild tulip, *Tulipa grengiolensis*, which comes in yellow, yellow with red stripe, and red varieties. In fields above the village, 3500 bulbs bloom every May attracting visitors to a tulip festival in the village square.

Turn L at beginning of village and follow winding road that contours along the hillside through meadows. Pass hamlets of Bädel and Ze Hyschere, and in hamlet of Bänna turn sharply R on road that zigzags downhill round four hairpins. Continue descending through woods and after two more hairpins reach Rhone at **Filet** bridge (18km, 760m) (accommodation, refreshments, camping). Cross river and turn L on main road (Furkastrasse, route 19).

Road route via Lax avoiding rough descent into Binntal
From road junction in centre of Ernen, fork R (Uber-Hengert, sp Brig) downhill out of village. Follow road round two hairpin bends through Niederernen. Cross bridge over Rhone and start ascending. After 250m, shortly before hairpin bend, bear L on path (footpath sign) away from road. Continue onto quiet road and follow this uphill under railway bridge to reach main road (route 19). Turn L and continue uphill through **Lax** (41km, 1042m) (accommodation, refreshments, station).

Follow main road through Deisch with railway L, then descend round two hairpin bends. After bend R, turn sharply L (sp Grengiols) downhill away from main road over entrance to railway tunnel round two more hairpins. Cross Rhone then turn R at T-junction and continue through fields passing below Grengiols L to reach main road. Bear L and follow road past Bettmeralp cable car station L (46km, 823m) (camping, station). Continue on main road with railway L and Rhone R to pass **Filet** bridge L (48.5km, 760m) (accommodation, refreshments, camping) where routes combine.

Combined route continues

From Filet follow main road (Furkastrasse) over railway crossing to reach **Mörel** (49km/56km, 764m) (accommodation, refreshments, tourist office, station). ▶

> From Mörel two cable cars carry passengers up to the car-free village of **Riederalp**, high above the north side of the valley, from where further cable cars head up to Hohfluh and Moosfluh. Here there are spectacular views of the Aletsch, Europe's longest glacier, which runs down for 24km from the south face of Jungfrau. The Aletsch Arena ski resort around Riederalp and Bettmeralp takes its name from this glacier.

Continue following main road past cable car station R and on past quarries R. Pass Hohflue chapel R and after 250 turn L on cycle track. Cross railway and turn R following track parallel with railway to reach **Bitsch** (station). Pass station R and turn R under railway, then turn sharply L to continue on cycle track beside railway. Cross bridge over river Massa and immediately turn sharply R downhill. ▶ Turn R again under bridge and bear R beside point where Massa and Rhone merge. Follow riverbank track under road bridge and pass **Naters** R (accommodation, refreshments), with extensive railway yards of Brig across river L.

Furkastrasse is a busy main road with no cycle lane.

The Massa carries meltwaters from the Aletsch glacier down to the Rhone.

The ossuary in Naters has a wall of skulls

Although **Naters** (pop 10,300) is a separate munici-
pality, it is in reality a part of Brig north of the Rhone.
At its core is an attractive village, older than Brig, of
old wooden houses surrounding St Mauritius parish
church and its nearby ossuary, with a wall covered
entirely by skulls. Clearly visible on the hillside
west of Naters is an old fortress that now houses a
museum of the Papal Swiss Guard, the mercenary
'army' of the Vatican and protectors of the Pope,
many of whom were recruited from this area.

The stage ends at Rottubrigga bridge (55.5km/62.5km,
671m) which links Naters with **Brig** (accommodation,
refreshments, camping, tourist office, cycle shop, station)
on opposite side of river.

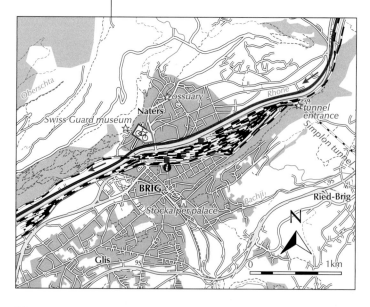

BRIG

Stockalper Palace in Brig was home to one of 17th-century Europe's richest men

Brig (pop 13,200) owes its prosperity to its position at the foot of the Simplon pass, which is the most accessible pass over the Alps and links the Rhone and Po basins. In medieval times the pass was crossed by mule trains and Brig grew up to serve the traders' needs. The town's most prominent building, Stockalper Palace, was built by Kaspar von Stockalper (1609–1691), a merchant whose control of the pass and domination of the salt trade enabled him to become one of Europe's richest men. Part of the palace was used as a salt warehouse. His motto *Sospes lucra carpat*, which translates as 'Keep safe the profit taker', is an anagram of his name in Latin, Caspar Stocalperus. He was, however, a major local benefactor, endowing monasteries, churches, schools and houses in Brig.

The first road pass was built by Napoléon between 1801–1805 to facilitate his invasion of Italy and retains the name 'Route Napoléon'. The modern road still uses part of this old route. The first rail tunnel opened in 1906 and the second bore in 1921. They were upgraded during the late 1990s to take piggyback freight trains and high-speed passenger trains as part of the NEAT (New Alpine Transit) project.

STAGE 2
Brig to Sierre

Start	Brig (Naters), Rottubrigga bridge (671m)
Finish	Sierre/Siders, Rue du Bourg (541m)
Distance	41km
Waymarking	Rhone route R1

Leaving Goms and entering the upper Valais, the Rhone becomes a recognisable river rather than a fast-flowing mountain stream. The route follows the valley as far as Leuk, either on the riverbank or on quiet roads through nearby fields. Between Leuk and Sierre the river has cut an unstable gorge through a moraine. Here the route follows a main road over the moraine away from the river, and then descends into Sierre. The going is level to Leuk then has a slight climb over the moraine and a fast descent to Sierre.

Note the outside balconies allowing the chickens access to fresh air.

From Rottubrigga bridge in **Naters** follow cycle track W beside riverside road (Mühleweg). Bear L onto Kiesweg still following Rhone. After 100m fork L under railway bridge along riverside road past industrial area R and poultry farm. ◄ Continue beside river with

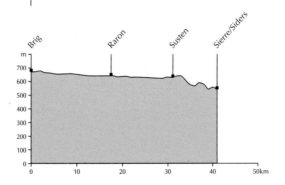

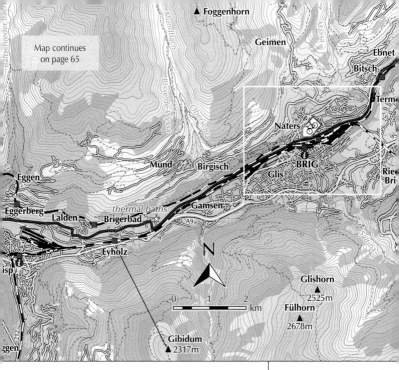

Map continues
on page 65

original Lötschberg railway line above (and steadily gaining height) R. Continue onto wider road (Erlenweg) and after 2km turn R (sp Brigerbad Bad) to reach Brigerbad thermal baths (camping). By entrance to baths, turn L (Thermalbadstrasse) and follow this to centre of **Brigerbad** (6km, 652m) (accommodation, refreshments).

Bear R before Romerhof hotel (Badhaltestrasse) and cycle out of village. At major junction turn R (Zum Kreuz) into **Lalden** (accommodation and camping in Eyholz across river, station). Fork L at next junction (Zenstadeln) and R at crossroads (Sandstrasse). Turn L at T-junction (Bachstrasse) and after 250m fork R on cycle track with hillside rising R. Pass sports field and bear R onto road (Finnubach), passing Lonza-DSM biopharmaceutical factory L which produces vitamins and fragrances and is the largest employer in Visp.

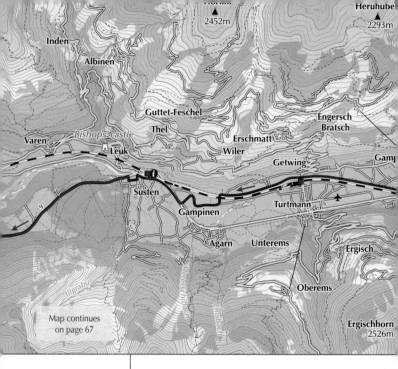

Map continues
on page 67

The **valley behind Visp** that runs south into the
mountains leads to Saas Fee and the car-free resort
of Zermatt. Towering over Zermatt is the Matterhorn.
Although this cannot be seen from the Rhone valley, another mountain, Dom (4545m), which rises
above Saas Fee and is the highest mountain entirely
in Switzerland, can be seen above the valley. Also
in this valley is the Visperterminen vineyard, the
highest in Europe at 1150m, which produces white
wine from Heida and Traminer grapes.

Just before this road bears L towards river, fork R on
cycle track (Taleya) alongside drainage ditch. Where this
ends in Kumme (9km, 651m), turn R (sp Ausserberg).
Cross Baltscheider Bach stream and turn sharply L and
immediately R (Kreuzmattenstrasse).

Follow road back to Rhone and cross river. Turn L and bear R under railway and motorway then cross bridge over slip road and turn R at T-junction. Fork L through fields, then turn L and R past stables. Continue past farms and turn R on side road beside main road. ▶ Follow track as it turns R away from road and turn L opposite heliport entrance. Turn R at second cross-roads (St Germanerstrasse) and go ahead across disued runway of old airfield. ▶ Continue under motorway and railway, then bear L over Rhone and L again along oppo-site riverbank. Continue to reach Raron bridge and turn R (Bahnhofstrasse) into **Raron** (17.5km, 638m) (accom-modation, refreshments, tourist office, station).

The attractive village of **Raron** (pop 1950) sits beneath the 16th-century hilltop church of

The paddock beside the track is the site of 'cow-fighting' contests held every spring and autumn.

Raron military airfield, which opened in 1940, closed in 1994 after the end of the Cold War.

St Michael's Church, bored into a hillside in Raron, is the largest underground church in Europe

St Romanus. This was built to replace an earlier church in the valley that had been destroyed by floods in 1494. By the 20th century, containment of the river had removed the risk of flooding and in 1974 a new church was built below the hill. St Michael's, which is bored into the cliffs of the hillside and holds 500 worshippers, is the largest underground church in Europe. The carillon over the entrance was added in 1982.

Turn L in centre of village and follow Stadelmatten-strasse past quarry R to reach **Niedergestein** (refreshments). Turn L in village (Obergeschstrasse) and R at crossroads (Hauptstrasse). After house 63, turn L at crossroads (Rottustrasse) and follow this out of village to reach Rhone. Turn R along gravel riverside track and cross railway. Continue to reach Gampel Steg bridge (22.5km, 630m) (station; accommodation, refreshments, camping in Gampel 1km off-route).

Pass under bridge then dog-leg R and L to cross river Lonza and return to Rhone riverbank. Continue beside river L on gravel track. Pass under **Getwing** road bridge then turn L at next bridge, crossing river, railway and motorway and bear R (Industriestrasse) with golf course L. Follow Industriestrasse as it bears R through small industrial estate. Immediately past last factory, turn L through fields (Treichgässi) gently uphill to **Gampinen** (accommodation, refreshments). Turn R and continue out of village beside main road (route 9) L. Dog-leg L and R under road then pass roundabout and continue on cycle track L of road to reach **Susten** (31.5km, 632m) (accommodation, refreshments, camping, tourist office, Leuk station). ▶

Fork L before roundabout and follow Sustenstrasse ahead through town centre. Turn L (Pletschenstrasse, sp Pletschen) uphill then turn R (Brückenmatte). Turn R (Waldstrasse) at T-junction to reach main road and turn L uphill out of town using cycle lane R. Follow main road for 6.5km as it climbs slightly over a moraine then descends through **Pfynwald** forest (camping) to reach a motorway junction. Just before start of motorway, bear R away from main road on cycle track through scrubland and turn R (sp Sierre) beside road linking Sierre to motorway. At roundabout cross side road then drop down to turn L under main road. After subway, turn R and immediately fork L (Rte

Although Leuk station is situated in Susten, the small town of Leuk is a steep 1.75km away, north of the Rhone.

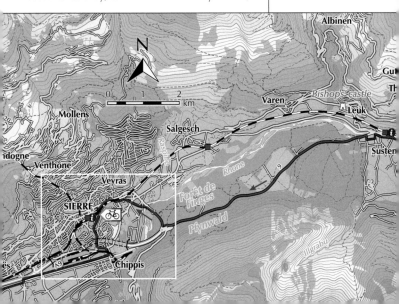

du Bois de Finges) on quiet road parallel with main road. Cross old Rhone bridge and go ahead to reach roundabout. Continue ahead (still Rte de Bois de Finges) and follow road bearing L. Where this ends, continue ahead on cycle track beside railway and turn R over railway (Ch du Monastère). Turn L (Rte du Simplon) on cycle lane R. Fork L (sp Chippis, still Rte du Simplon) to reach junction with Rue du Bourg just before St Catherine's Church near to centre of **Sierre** (41km, 541m) (accommodation, refreshments, camping, tourist office, cycle shop, station).

SIERRE/SIDERS

Sierre/Siders (pop 16,800) owes its joint name to its position close to the language boundary between German-speaking and francophone Switzerland, which runs over the moraine east of the town. This was originally the boundary between German-speaking Alemanni and French-speaking Burgundians, a division that has lasted for 1600 years. As a result, Sierre is an officially bilingual town, one of only three in Switzerland, although in reality everyone here speaks French. The forest on the moraine, which is known as Pfynwald on the eastern side and Forêt de Finges on the west, is a protected area and is regarded as one of the most scientifically important pine forests in Europe. Sierre marks the start of the Valais wine-growing region, which extends along the north side of the valley almost to

The funicular between Sierre/Siders and Crans-Montana is the world's longest

Lake Geneva. There is a wine museum in a former château, and a wine path meandering through vineyards to the well-preserved village of Salgesh where there is a viniculture museum dedicated to the growing of grapes. High on the valley side, north of Sierre, you can see the up-market ski resort of Crans-Montana. This is linked to Sierre by a modern funicular, with the world's longest cable, that takes 12min to climb 927m to the resort 4km away.

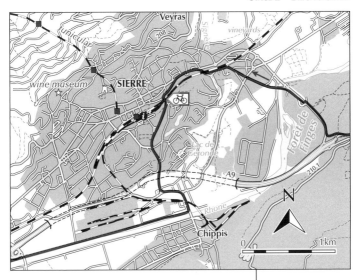

Sierre/Siders town hall

STAGE 3
Sierre to Martigny

Start	Sierre/Siders, Rue du Bourg (541m)
Finish	Martigny, Branson bridge (455m)
Distance	44.5km
Waymarking	Rhone route R1

Now in French-speaking lower Valais, the Rhone flows south west through a classically straight glacial valley. The valley floor is filled with orchards while the south-facing valley side is covered with terraced vineyards. Apart from two small diversions, one of which passes through Sion, cantonal capital of Valais, the completely level cycle route follows the riverbank throughout.

From junction between Rte du Simplon and Rue du Bourg near centre of **Sierre**, follow Rte de la Plaine SE (sp Chippis) under railway bridge. Continue ahead over roundabout (still Rte de la Plaine) and bear R into Rte de Sous-Géronde. Turn L at second roundabout and R at third (still Rte de Sous-Géronde). Cross railway level crossing and turn R beside Novelis factory (do not cross river) on Ch des Peupliers parallel with Rhone.

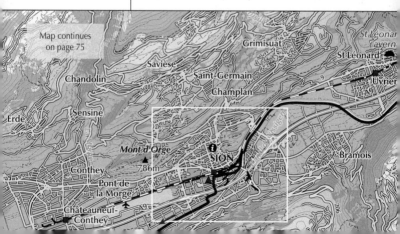

Map continues on page 75

Pass under first road bridge then turn L across river on next bridge and R along opposite bank on flood dyke, which is followed for 11km. Pass series of large grassy mounds L, the restored spoil tips of aluminium smelter that formerly stood on this site. Pass under road bridge then beside Sierre golf club to reach next road bridge (12km, 504m). Our route continues along the riverbank but you could turn L to reach **Bramois** (camping) or R, across river, to visit **Uvrier** (accommodation, refreshments, cycle shop, station). ▸

Continue along riverbank and pass under motorway bridge. Cross bridge over side stream and turn R at

In Uvrier (2.5km from cycle route) is St Léonard's cavern, the largest subterranean lake in Europe, where visitors can take a 30min boat trip around the lake.

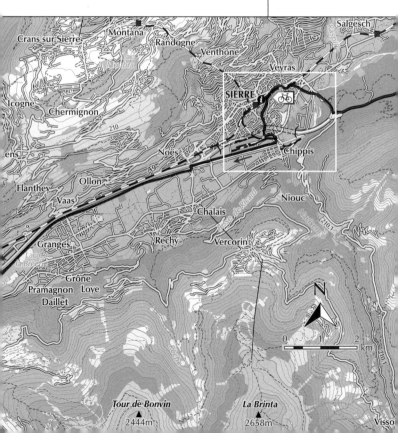

Boat trips can be taken on the underground lake in St Léonard's cavern near Ulvrier

To reach the centre of Sion, turn right at the roundabout and continue over a railway bridge.

T-junction to continue beside Rhone, past Sion golf club and under another road bridge. Turn R across Rhone on combined cycle/pedestrian bridge and L on gravel track along opposite bank. Emerge onto road to reach roundabout in **Sion** (17.5km, 495m) (accommodation, refreshments, youth hostel, tourist office, cycle shop, station). ◀

Continue ahead onto Rue de l'Industrie and follow this, bearing R, to reach roundabout at rear of Sion

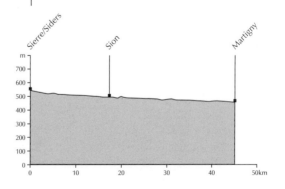

SION

Sion (pop 35,000), the cantonal capital of Valais, has an old centre surrounded by a modern Swiss city. On a rise above the Rhone, and dominated by a craggy hill, Sion has been inhabited since Mesolithic times. The Romans built a town on the site and when they converted to Christianity, Sion became the site of the first bishopric north of the Alps. A cathedral was built in the sixth century and by the 11th century the Prince-Bishop of Sion controlled all of Valais. During medieval times the city was often embroiled in conflict between neighbouring states, resulting in the construction of four castles and substantial fortifications. Two castles, Tourbillon and Valère, overlook the city from adjacent hills and both are open to visitors. The church in Valère castle contains the oldest playable organ in the world. In the city centre the most notable buildings are the cathedral, St Théodule church, the town hall with an astronomical clock and the Supersaxo house (1503) with a lavishly decorated great hall.

station. Turn L (Rue des Champs-de-Tabac), then go ahead at next roundabout, pass under motorway and bear R (Rte de la Drague) through industrial area. After 300m,

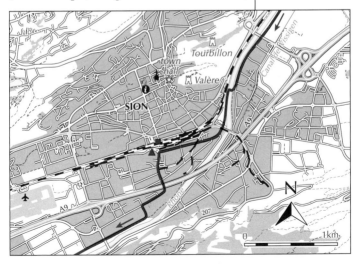

The left turn is
easy to miss.

turn L on small side road between industrial buildings
and bear R along Ch des Gardes-de-Nuit parallel with
Rhone. ◄ Pass under road bridge and fork immediately L,
climbing steeply through bollards, and continue on cycle
track along flood dyke, which soon becomes gravel. Dog-
leg R and L to emerge onto road and continue on riverbank past **Aproz** bridge (23km, 485m) (refreshments,
camping, station).

Continue along riverbank, crossing bridge over side
stream and bearing L beside river. Cross railway level

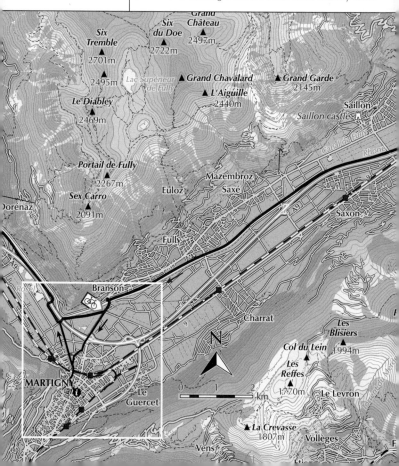

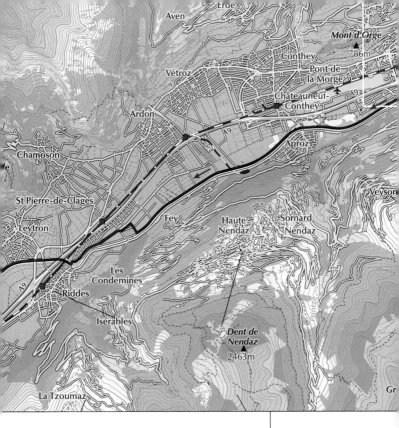

crossing and continue beside river to reach large electricity sub-station R. Turn R away from river just before substation through orchards, then L at T-junction continuing beside drainage canal. Dog-leg R and L over canal and continue on other side through more orchards to reach T-junction. Turn L past aggregates depot L to reach **Riddes** bridge (31km, 476m) (station).

Turn R on cycle track beside river (do not cross bridge). Pass under railway bridge and fork L under motorway. Continue along riverbank with distant view of Saillon castle on hillside R. Pass six bridges and village of **Fully** R (41km, 465m) (accommodation, refreshments)

MARTIGNY

Batiaz castle above Martigny controls the entrance to three Alpine passes

Martigny (pop 18,300) sits near the confluence of the Dranse and Rhone rivers, where the Rhone turns 90 degrees to head north towards Lake Geneva. Originally a Gaulish settlement, it was developed by the Romans into an important town by the entrance to the Forclaz (to Chamonix, France) and Great-St-Bernhard (to Aosta, Italy) passes, in addition to the route following the Rhone to Brig and the Simplon pass. The medieval Château de la Batiaz controls the road leading to these passes. Roman remains include a restored amphitheatre, which is used for traditional cow-fights and modern-day performances. For most of the medieval period, the town was in French (Burgundian or Savoyard) hands, only becoming part of Switzerland after the fall of Napoléon (1815). Martigny-Bourg is the oldest part of town, with picturesque old houses and artisans' workshops. The very modern Fondation Pierre Gianadda houses a museum and art gallery. It was established by Leonard Gianadda in honour of his brother Pierre who was killed in an air crash in Italy. Across a road and connected by a tunnel is a motor museum with a large collection of early Swiss-built cars. Surrounding the Fondation is a sculpture park with works by Giacometti, Modigliani, Rodin and Toulouse-Lautrec. Near to the amphitheatre is a museum and kennels dedicated to the St Bernhard pass and the iconic dogs that take their name from the pass. The mountains around the town hold a number of popular ski resorts, the most well-known being Verbier, 12km east of Martigny.

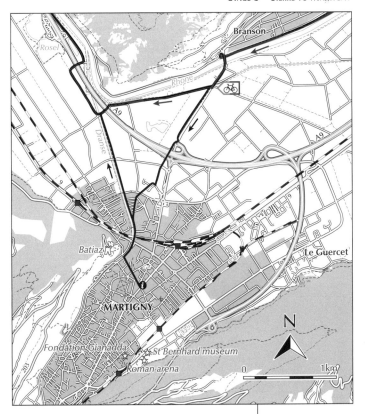

to reach road beside **Branson** bridge (accommodation). Follow track bearing R away from river and immediately R at roundabout to cross Rhone (cycle track R). Continue for 400m, past aggregates depot R and over irrigation canal, to reach crossroads (44.5km, 455m). ▶

Turn right to start Stage 4, or continue ahead to reach Martigny (accommodation, refreshments, camping, tourist office, cycle shop, station) after 2.5km.

STAGE 4
Martigny to St Gingolph

Start	Martigny (Branson bridge) (455m)
Finish	St Gingolph, boat pier (384m)
Distance	44.5km
Waymarking	Rhone route R1 to Le Bouveret, then Tour de Léman R46

Now heading north, the Rhone, still in a deep straight glacial valley, soon leaves Valais and enters Vaud canton. Apart from two short deviations, one over a moraine and the other through the centre of St Maurice, the cycle route follows the riverbank all the way to the shore of Lake Geneva before ending at the Swiss/French border. This stage is generally flat, except for a 50m climb over the moraine.

From crossroads on road leading from **Martigny** to Branson bridge, 2.5km N of town, follow quiet road W parallel with irrigation canal. Pass stables L and continue on narrow cycle track. Emerge beside road and after 200m turn L under motorway (Rte du Verney). Cross river Dranse and turn immediately R through orchards. At point where asphalt surface ahead ends, turn R under

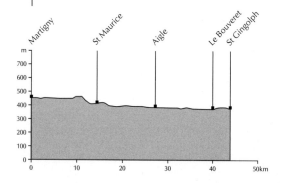

Map continues
on page 82

(Plans-sur-Bex)
2294m
Pointe d'Euzanne
2320m
2482m

National-Redoubt

Augustinian abbey

Lavey
Village

*Dent
Favre*
2917m

Vérossaz

St Maurice

*Pointe
des Martinets*
2653m

Mex

Lavey-
les-Bains

Morcles

*Glacier des
Martinets*
2969m

Tita Sèri
2850m

La
Rasse

Evionnaz

*Six
du Doe*
2722m

*Six
Tremble*
2701m

Collonges

*Lac Supérieur
de Fully*

chers de
agnerie
00m

*Labyrinthe
Adventure*

La Balmaz

Le Diâbley
2469m

Salantin
2482m

Portail de Fully
2267m

Sex Carro
2091m

Miéville

Dorénaz

de
fe

*Sex des
Granges*
2082m

Vernayaz

*Petits
Perrons*
2616m
*Le
Luisin*
2785m

Les
Granges

Branson

A9

Salvan

N

Les
Marécottes

*Mont de
la Barme*
a   2307m
arme

Le Trétien

0   1   2
km

Ravoire

MARTIGNY

*Le
Guercet*

2m

La Fontaine

21

ST MAURICE

St Maurice castle and old bridge

St Maurice (pop 4500) takes its name from an early Christian martyr who was killed by the Romans. An abbey bearing his name was built by the Burgundians (AD515) on the site of the tomb of St Theodore, first bishop of Valais, which is the oldest Christian site in Switzerland. It became an Augustinian monastery in 1128. Rebuilt several times since then, its most treasured artefact is a drinking goblet from the second century BC. The town's position in a narrow canyon below a moraine led to a bridge being built in the 12th century (the first above Lake Geneva) and subsequently to construction of a castle and fortifications. These were steadily enhanced and by the Second World War they were a key part of the National Redoubt, a defensive line across Switzerland aimed at denying an aggressor access to the Alpine passes. The extensive works consisted of barracks, gun positions, hospitals, and command posts tunnelled into the mountains on both sides of the valley. They remained actively manned until after the end of the Cold War, with decommissioning starting in 1995. Parts of the fortifications are now open as a tourist attraction.

motorway then L alongside irrigation ditch. Continue beside motorway L to reach river Trient. Turn R then L over river and continue alongside Rhone to reach road bridge that links **Vernayaz** L (accommodation, refreshments, station) and **Dorénaz** R (5km, 454m).

Dog-leg L and R across road, then bear R to continue along riverbank with motorway L. After 2km, dog-leg L and R over sidestream then continue for another 2.5km. ▸ Pass bridge R leading across Rhone to **Collonges** and bridge L over railway into **Evionnaz** (9km, 455m) (station). After 300m turn L under railway line and R on cycle track beside main road (route 9), becoming cycle lane. Ascend slightly then descend past campsite R (camping) and through woods over small moraine. Where road reaches motorway junction L, bear R parallel with flyover and drop down onto Ch de la Choume to reach Rte des Bains (accommodation, refreshments in Lavey-les-Bains across Rhone). Cross over then turn immediately L (Ch de l'Ile d'Epines) and follow this bearing R beside motorway slip road. Just before motorway overbridge, turn R and L along riverside cycle track (Promenade du Rhône). After 700m, cross small bridge and turn immediately L (Promenade du Mauvoisin) beside Mauvoisin stream. Turn first R (Ch des Iles) and follow this street bearing L under main road and R to emerge on Ave du Simplon. Continue into centre of **St Maurice** (14.5km, 419m) (accommodation, refreshments, tourist office, station).

Bear L at beginning of town centre (Ave de la Gare) and immediately R (Ave d'Agaune). Pass Augustinian abbey L and continue ahead over roundabout out of town (Rte du Chablais) with wooded hillside rising L and Rhone R to reach St Maurice castle in narrowest part of gorge L and 12th-century bridge R. ▸ Continue beside main road for 250m, then turn L under railway bridge and bear R (Ch de St Maurice) beside railway. Emerge onto road and follow this over level crossing. Turn immediately L on cycle track, then cross main road and continue between fields to reach Rhone. Turn L beside river and continue on riverside cycle track to **Massongex**

Just before Evionnaz, on the opposite side of the motorway, is Labyrinthe Adventure, the world's largest maze with 3km of paths designed to replicate Valais canton.

Part-way up the hillside on the left is the entrance to La Grotte aux Fées, an underground lake fed by a waterfall.

Map continues
on page 85

(18km, 398m) (refreshments, station; accommodation, cycle shop in Bex across river).

On opposite side of Rhone, just north of **Bex**, are extensive salt mines. A small train that runs into the mine through a network of tunnels allows visitors to see the old workings. Although the mine is still active, nowadays salt is extracted by pumping water into the salt deposit from above and collecting the brine slurry that emerges below. This is piped across the Rhone to chemical works in Monthey where it is used as a feedstock to produce chlorine and caustic soda.

Opposite Massongex pedestrian/cycle bridge over Rhone, turn L away from river and immediately R on road through riverside car park. Fork R on cycle track along flood dyke beside river. Drop down under road bridge, passing **Monthey** (refreshments, station) L then continue on flood dyke for 4km. Dog-leg R and L under next road bridge passing **Collombey** (refreshments, station) L. Pass oil refinery L and under pipe bridge connecting this with railhead on opposite side of Rhone. Continue past **Illarsaz** (27.5km, 389m) L, where a pedestrian/cycle bridge gives access to **Aigle** (accommodation, refreshments, tourist office, station) on opposite side of river.

Aigle (pop 10,500) is a major centre for the Swiss wine industry. A much-rebuilt 11th-century Savoyard castle, one of the most attractive in Switzerland, stands surrounded by vineyards outside the town. After use as the governor's residence during a period of Bernese control, it was for many years a prison. Restoration work since 1972 has converted the castle into a museum of vines and wine, including the world's largest collection of wine labels, with state rooms used for formal dinners. Aigle is the jumping-off point for a number of small ski resorts and three mountain railways climb into the mountains both east and west of the valley.

Aigle château has a wine museum and is surrounded by vineyards

Turn R over bridge
to follow Stages 5A
and 6A around the N
side of Lake Geneva.

Continue on riverside cycle track (do not cross river) under another road bridge and pass **Vouvry** (32.5km, 378m) (accommodation, refreshments, station). Dog-leg L and R across approach road to Porte-du-Sciex bridge, then pass under next bridge before reaching pedestrian/cycle bridge over Rhone at Le Bouveret (38km, 375m). ◄

Continue ahead along flood dyke beside Rhone. Turn L just before leisure pool complex and emerge onto road. Go ahead over lifting bridge passing marina R and Swiss Vapeur Park L into **Le Bouveret** (40km, 374m) (accommodation, refreshments, camping, tourist office, station).

Swiss Vapeur Park is a miniature railway complex with ride-on carriages pulled by small steam engines that wind through extensive grounds, passing under tunnels and over viaducts.

Bear R passing between station L and marina R. Pass very small RAF Lancaster memorial R and opposite landing stage for Lake Geneva boat services turn L over railway crossing. Turn L and immediately R (Rue du Lac), bearing L steeply uphill. Turn sharply R onto main road (Rte Cantonale), continuing to ascend. Follow road out of village past pink-coloured César Ritz catering college L and continue above lakeshore. Cross railway level crossing to reach **St Gingolph** (44.5km, 384m) (accommodation, refreshments, station). Opposite entrance to station, fork L (Rue du Port) downhill to reach stage end beside Lake Geneva boat service pier.

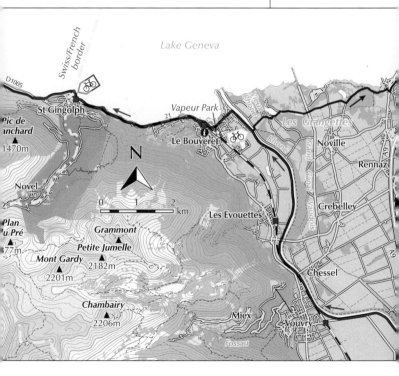

85

STAGE 5A
Le Bouveret to Morges

Start	Le Bouveret bridge (374m)
Finish	Morges, Temple de Morges church (373m)
Distance	50km
Waymarking	Rhone route R1, Tour de Léman R46

Circling the north side of Lake Geneva, after Vevey the route climbs steeply away from the lakeshore through the affluent residential areas and terraced vineyards of Lavaux. Dropping back downhill, the route passes below the Olympic city of Lausanne and continues close to the lake before ending in Morges. The undulating 14km between Vevey and Lutry is the hilliest part of the whole route.

Cycle E over **Le Bouveret** bridge and turn L along opposite riverbank. After 75m, turn R and follow waymarked track winding through Les Grangettes, crossing Vieux Rhône and passing Port du Vieux-Rhône marina. Continue over Grand Canal Vaudois then turn L at T-junction on road through woodland. Turn R alongside another canal, then cross main road and turn immediately L over second

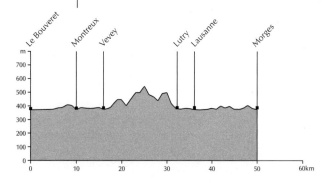

Map continues
on page 95

Mont Chesau
982m

Mont Pèlerin
tower ☆ ▲
1080m

Attalens

Mont Vuarat
985m

Le
Foll
1730

Chardonne   Jongny   Chevalleyres

Corsier-   A9
sur-Vevey   St Légier-La Chiésaz

Corseaux

VEVEY   Blonay

                                            Brent
La Tour-de-Peilz

                                            Fontanivent

Burier   Chernex

                        Clarens   Glion
                                                    Caux

                                    MONTREUX

                                    Territet
                                    Veytaux

Lake Geneva

N

0   1   2
|——|——|——|——| km

                                    Chillon

Swiss/French
border

                                            Villeneuve

                        Vieux-Rhône   Les Grangettes

                ph

                Le Bouveret   vapeur
                               park   Noville
                                                 Rennaz

                Port Valais

WITZERLAND   Crebelley
                                                        Roche

Les Grangettes delta where the Rhone enters Lake Geneva

Grand-Rue is a cobbled one-way street with contra-flow allowed for cyclists.

bridge. Follow Grand-Rue into **Villeneuve** (5km, 374m) (accommodation, refreshments, camping, tourist office, station). ◄

Pass station then bear R onto main road (route 9), cross railway bridge and continue parallel with railway past Château de Chillon.

Built in the 11th century, **Château de Chillon** became home to the Counts of Savoy. It was never captured but did change hands (1536) after a siege, coming under the control of the Bernese.

Its modern-day popularity is partly down to Lord Byron who visited in 1816 and wrote a poem, 'The Prisoner of Chillon', about François de Bonivard who was imprisoned beneath the castle from 1530–1536. Many visitors wrongly assume that Byron was imprisoned here. He wasn't, but he did (allegedly) carve his name in the dungeon. The castle has been extensively renovated, and great halls, bedrooms, courtyards and dungeons are all open to visitors. It is reached by a drawbridge over a short stretch of natural water that acts like a moat protecting the castle.

Follow main road past **Territet** (accommodation, refreshments, YH, station). Then pass under railway bridge into Ave du Casino and drop down to Pl du Marché on lakeside in centre of **Montreux** (10km, 384m) (accommodation, refreshments, tourist office, cycle shop, station).

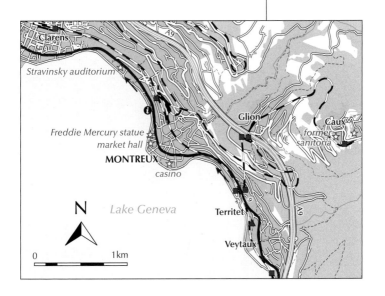

MONTREUX

Montreux (pop 26,000) is an up-market resort town on the shores of Lake Geneva with Rochers de Naye (2045m) rising behind. Despite settlement that started in Roman times and a wine industry that dates from the 12th century, Montreux remained a small impoverished community until the 19th century. Health tourism, with wealthy clients drawn to Montreux for a climate said to benefit those suffering from consumption (TB) and the arrival of railways that enabled them to reach the area from northern Europe, established Montreux as a popular resort prior to 1914. Large sanatoria on the hillsides serviced these wealthy patrons. The First World War spelt disaster for Montreux. Fighting across the continent prevented guests from reaching Switzerland and the area struggled throughout the war and inter-war period. Moreover, developments in health care meant 'Swiss mountain air' was no longer the remedy for wealthy patients with TB.

Like other parts of Switzerland, Montreux was saved by the Swiss banking system with its high level of secrecy and low level of taxation that drew in foreign capital and wealthy refugees from across Europe, particularly soviet Russia and Nazi Germany. After the Second World War, Montreux again became a popular resort and residential area for better-off Europeans. However, today there are only half the number of hotels compared to 1912.

The town has a casino and holds annual music, television and advertising festivals. The jazz festival is held in the Stravinsky auditorium, named after the composer who lived in Montreux (1910–1915) where he wrote some of his best-known compositions including 'Petrushka' and 'The Rite of Spring'. Among more recent residents, one of the best known was Freddie Mercury, vocalist with the pop-music group Queen, who spent some time in Montreux before his death in 1991. He is commemorated with a statue by the market hall.

Villeneuve, Montreux, Clarens, La Tour-de-Peilz and Vevey form one continuous built-up area with a trolleybus line running from Villeneuve to Vevey.

Continue on Grand Rue past boat landing stage then complex of exhibition halls and Stravinsky auditorium that host Montreux's various festivals, into **Clarens** (accommodation, refreshments, station). ◀ Pass marina and continue on main road through **Burier** (camping, station). At beginning of **La Tour-de-Peilz**, turn L (sp Port), then R at first T-junction and L at second. Pass castle then bear R along lakeside. La Tour-de-Peilz Château houses a

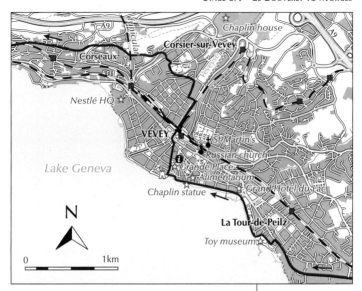

museum dedicated to toys and games. Continue through Jardin Roussy riverside gardens, then bear L between marina and Grand Hôtel du Lac beside Quai Perdonnet. Pass Alimentarium museum and Charlie Chaplin statue to reach Grande Pl in **Vevey** (17km, 379m) (accommodation, refreshments, camping, tourist office, cycle shop, station).

VEVEY

Vevey (pop 20,000) is the principal town of the Lavaux wine region. There is a museum of wine and every 20 years (once per generation; the last was in 2019) a spectacular wine growers' festival is held in Grande Place. On Saturday mornings during July and August a folklorique market is held where you can taste a different wine village's output each week. Just buy an empty glass and have it filled as many times as you like.

Vevey is home to Nestlé, one of the world's largest food companies. Henri Nestlé pioneered powdered milk in 1867 and in 1875 milk chocolate was invented by the company. Nestlé's modernist worldwide headquarters are at the west end of town. The Alimentarium, a museum of food and nutrition, is supported by the company. Other buildings include a Russian orthodox church built to serve an expatriate community. La Grenette, formerly a grain market, and Château de l'Aile both overlook the large market square of Grande Place.

The town's attractive position and mild climate have lured famous residents for centuries. After the death of Oliver Cromwell, two of those responsible for the execution of King Charles I fled to Vevey. One of them (Andrew Broughton) is buried in St Martin's churchyard. Thackeray, Dostoyevsky, Hemingway, Henry James and Arnold Bennett all wrote books while living here. The Grand Hôtel du Lac was the inspiration for Anita Brookner's Booker prize winning novel Hotel du Lac.

Leave Grande Pl by NW corner to reach Pl de la Gare. Turn R across main road then pass station R and go under railway bridge. Turn L over river Veveyse and second R (Rue des Moulins). ◀ At complicated six-way road junction, turn half-L passing car park for Nestlé employees L, then fork R uphill past Parc Charlie Chaplin into **Corsier-sur-Vevey** (accommodation, refreshments).

Rue des Moulins is one-way with a contra-flow cycle lane.

Turn L at T-junction in village centre and continue ahead over main road at staggered crossroads. Pass vineyards and cross funicular to reach **Corseaux** (accommodation, refreshments, station).

The UNESCO-listed **Lavaux vineyards**, which cover 800ha and stretch for 10km along terraced hillsides from Corseaux to Lutry, cover every available metre and run right down to the lakeside; even the railway embankments are planted with vines! Principal grape varieties are chasselas (white) and pinot noir (red).

Pass below oldest part of village, then fork R uphill. Continue over railway crossing and descend through vineyards to reach T-junction. Turn R uphill, then L on concrete track contouring through vineyards and passing

SIR CHARLIE CHAPLIN

Sir Charlie Chaplin (1889–1977) lived in Corsier for the last 24 years of his life. He was born in England and his childhood was one of poverty and hardship. He took up comic acting at an early age and moved to America aged 19 to tour with the Fred Karno company. In 1914 he started appearing in silent films and soon developed his 'little tramp' persona, which made him one of the world's best-known actors. As a co-founder of United Artists studios (1919) he was able to make his own films, sticking to the silent film format even when sound became available. From 1940, when he produced *The Great Dictator* satirising Adolf Hitler, his films became increasingly political bringing him into conflict with both the FBI and the House

After exclusion from America, Charlie Chaplin spent the rest of his life living near Vevey

Un-American Activities Committee which set out to expose alleged communist sympathisers in the American film industry. After making *Limelight* (1951) he left America for the premiere in London but while away his re-entry visa was cancelled. Choosing not to contest this decision he decided to settle in Switzerland and moved to Manoir de Ban in Corsier (1953). He did not return to America until 1972 when he visited Los Angeles to receive an honorary Oscar. He continued making films, now in England, but with decreasing success. As a British citizen he was knighted in 1975. After his death he was buried in Corsier cemetery but his coffin was dug-up and held for ransom. After it had been recovered it was buried again surrounded by reinforced concrete.

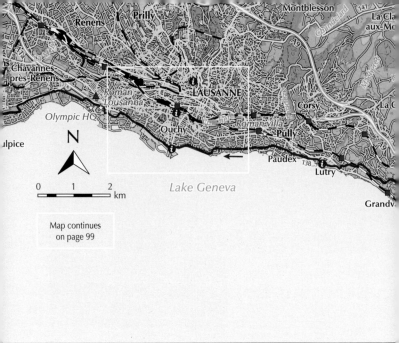

Map continues
on page 99

above wine-producing hamlet of **St Saphorin** (22km,
445m) (accommodation, refreshments, station).

Ascend through vineyards then bear R at T-junction
on asphalt track. Fork L at first junction and continue
below **Chexbres** (accommodation, refreshments, station).
Go ahead over two road crossings then wind downhill.
Turn R at T-junction and climb steeply for 300m to reach
main road at highest point of stage (545m, 175m above
Lake Geneva). Turn R downhill through **Epesses** (26.5km,
465m) (accommodation, refreshments, station) and **Riex**
(refreshments). Go ahead at roundabout (second exit),
climbing through vineyards and passing above **Cully**
(accommodation, refreshments, camping, tourist office,
station). Turn L at road junction (sp Lutry) and after 400m
fork L downhill through **Grandvaux** (29.5km, 492m)
(accommodation, refreshments, station).

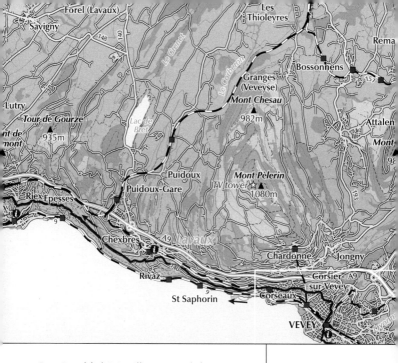

Bear R and fork L in village to reach five-way junction. Turn L onto main road winding downhill through Aran (refreshments) and Châtelard. Continue under railway bridge and turn immediately R. Bear L at junction of tracks then turn R at T-junction. Turn L at staggered crossroads then half-R (second exit) at roundabout. Continue into cobbled Grand-Rue through **Lutry** (32.5km, 380m) (accommodation, refreshments, tourist office, cycle shop, station).

Medieval **Lutry** (pop 10,500) began with an 11th-century abbey beside the lake. A small town grew up around this abbey, which was encircled by a defensive wall with a small castle. The abbey's monks planted vineyards outside the wall, heralding the beginning of viticulture in Lavaux. When the abbey closed (1537) local citizens took over the

Riverside gardens and château at Ouchy

vineyards, which they expanded steadily by replacing hillside forestry with vine terraces. From these beginnings vines have spread throughout Lavaux. Modern Lutry is a popular residential area for commuters to Lausanne.

A restored Roman villa at Prieuré in Pully (pop 16,700) contains a well-preserved Roman fresco showing a chariot race.

Pass sports ground, then bear L on main road and continue for 3km through **Paudex** and **Pully** (refreshments, cycle shop, station). ◄

Turn L at major road junction (sp Ouchy) and bear R along lakeside promenade. Pass Parc Olympique, with Olympic museum on hillside above, and continue past Beau Rivage palace R into centre of **Ouchy** on lakeshore below Lausanne (37km, 374m) (accommodation, refreshments, YH, camping, tourist office, cycle shop, station).

Bear L past metro station then continue parallel with lakeshore past marina and commercial port. Continue

LAUSANNE

Lausanne (pop 140,000 city, 308,000 metro) tiers down the hillside overlooking Lake Geneva. The Romans built a settlement on the lakeshore at Ouchy but, after this was destroyed by the Alemanni (AD379), subsequent development took place on the hill above where the cathedral stands. The city was part of the Holy Roman Empire (1032–1218) and was then controlled by the Savoyards (1218–1536) and Bernese (1536–1798) who were responsible for the adoption of Protestantism. It joined the Swiss Confederation in 1803.

Its attractive position and liberal politics attracted many writers and artists including Voltaire, Dickens (who wrote *Dombey and Son* here), Gibbon, Bennett, Southey and Eliot. In the 20th century the city became a centre for sports administration when first the International Olympic Committee (1915) and later the Court of Arbitration for Sport established headquarters here.

The cathedral was consecrated in 1275 when it held the coronation of Rudolph of Habsburg (who was Swiss) as Holy Roman Emperor, the first of a long line of Habsburgs who ruled the Holy Roman Empire until 1806. Regarded as the finest Gothic building in Switzerland, its main attractions include the southern (or Apostle's) doorway and the glass in the windows, some of which has been in place since the cathedral was built. The view from the tower overlooking the city, lake and snow-capped Alps is outstanding. The Château St Marie, originally the Bishops' palace, is now the cantonal government of Vaud, while the colossal Rumine palace houses the university administration and various museums.

The IOC headquarters are beside the lake at Vidy, west of the city, but the Olympic museum is southeast of the centre in a park overlooking the lake near Ouchy. Opened in 1993 it tells the story of the modern Olympics and was voted world museum of the year in 1995. A major refurbishment and extension has doubled the museum's size. The park surrounding the museum houses sport-related sculptures including works by Rodin.

ahead at two roundabouts, then pass tennis club and turn L (sp Port de Vidy). Wind through sports park, then turn R opposite entrance of Stade Pierre-de-Coubertin and bear L parallel with motorway. Pass ruins of Roman Lousonna, then campsite and HQ of International Olympic Committee. Follow road curving L and R to sewerage works R, then continue between allotments R and stele standing stone L. ▶ At end, bear L on cycle track beside

The stele commemorates Major Abraham Davel, a Vaudois patriot who was executed on this spot by the Bernese in 1723.

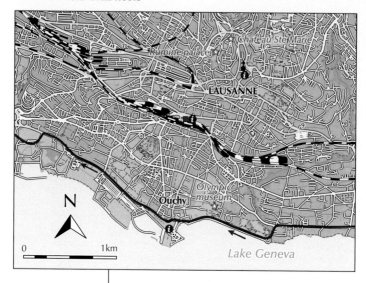

dual carriageway passing building with spire-like com-
munications mast on roof and other buildings of EPFL
including spectacular Rolex learning centre on opposite
side of road.

> **EPFL** (École Polytechnique Fédérale de Lausanne)
> is one of the world's top technological universities.
> Starting in the 19th century as part of Lausanne
> University, it then became a separate institution in
> 1969. The modern campus accommodates 20,000
> students, with facilities including a nuclear research
> reactor (Crocus) and the Rolex learning centre with
> areas for work, leisure and services.

Turn L away from main road at roundabout with
blue apple sculpture in middle and R at crossroads. Turn
L at T-junction and continue through **St Sulpice** (44km,
397m) (accommodation, refreshments, cycle shop).
Turn L opposite building 154 and continue to lakeside. Turn R beside lake past sports fields and fork L on

gravel track winding through woods. Cross bridge over river Venoge and turn L, then bear R on lakeside road to reach beginning of **Préverenges** (accommodation, refreshments).

Take second turning R and follow this winding through village. Turn L at crossroads and R uphill at next crossroads to reach main road. Turn L and continue downhill into **Morges** (50km, 373m) (accommodation, refreshments, camping, tourist office, cycle shop, station). Stage ends by Temple de Morges church L, at beginning of town centre one-way system.

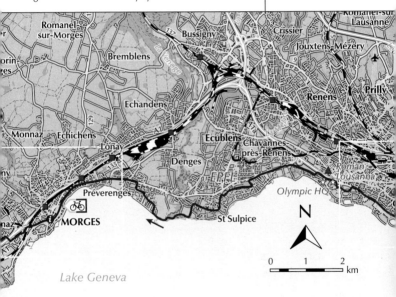

MORGES

The earliest settlement in Morges (pop 16,000) was of Bronze Age stilt houses on the lakeshore. Remains of the stilts and a dug-out canoe carved from oak (dated 1000BC) are in Geneva's archaeological museum. The medieval town started in 1286 with a castle built for Louis I of Savoy which dominates the port at the west end of town, and now houses a military and artillery museum. Other important buildings include the Auberge de la Croix Blanche (a medieval inn), the town hall of 1518, a granary, grammar school and various houses from the late 17th century that attest to the town's prosperity. The Temple de Morges church (1776) is a masterpiece of Swiss reformed church architecture.

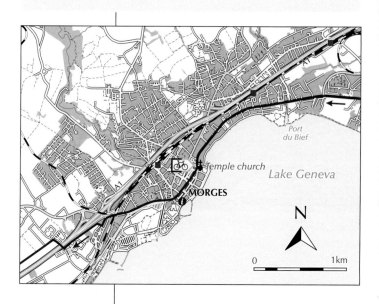

STAGE 6A

Morges to Geneva

Start	Morges, Temple de Morges church (373m)
Finish	Geneva, Pl de St Gervais (374m)
Distance	58km
Waymarking	Rhone route R1, Tour de Léman R46

This stage undulates gently between the shore of Lake Geneva and the terraced slopes of La Côte vineyards. The route passes a series of market towns, then the going becomes increasingly built-up before reaching the city of Geneva.

From Temple de **Morges** church, cycle S on Grand-Rue, passing many historic buildings including Auberge de la Croix Blanche and town hall. ▶ At end, cross Pl Charles Dufor and continue beside dual carriageway. Turn R at roundabout then pass under railway and turn L. ▶ Turn first R to reach T-junction and R under motorway. Turn first L through orchards then dog-leg R and L

Grand-Rue is pedestrianised with cycling permitted.

The left turn requires a difficult crossing of a busy main road.

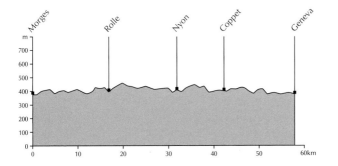

over staggered crossroads. Cross Boiron stream and wind through woods climbing to reach T-junction. Turn L, pass under motorway and fork immediately R. After 200m, bear L through fields downhill to reach railway. Turn R, then L under bridge. Go across main road and bear R along lakeshore passing marina. Go ahead into Rue du Pont-Levis to reach Pl de l'Horloge in **St Prex** (6km, 380m) (accommodation, refreshments, tourist office, station) with old gateway L.

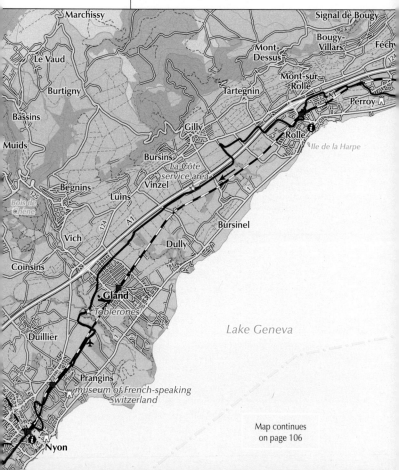

Map continues
on page 106

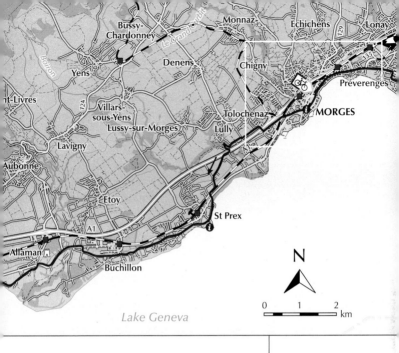

Lake Geneva

0 1 2 km

The old part of **St Prex** (pop 5750) sits on a small peninsula that was once closed-off by walls. All that remains of these walls is the main gateway topped by a clock tower. Some of the houses in Grand-Rue still display the wrought iron signs of the artisans that formerly occupied them.

Continue ahead and fork R uphill. After 300m fork L and continue out of village. Bear L at beginning of **Buchillon** (9km, 401m) (refreshments, station), then R on one-way street and continue out of village to reach roundabout. Turn L on main road and follow this to **Allaman** (11.5km, 405m) (accommodation, refreshments, station) with château above vineyard R. Turn L at crossroads then bear R through barriers onto gravel track. Emerge onto road and pass Allaman beach (refreshments). Where road ends continue ahead on cycle track through woods, then dog-leg L and R across main road. Continue past château

103

(behind walls R) into wine-producing village of **Perroy** (14km, 420m) (refreshments).

Bear L (Grand-Rue), passing church L. At end of village bear R and go ahead over crossroads. Cross railway bridge and turn immediately L. Turn R (on L of two parallel tracks) and follow concrete track as it bears L through fields to reach **Mont-sur-Rolle**. Turn R at beginning of village then L parallel with motorway. At T-junction, bear L then L again away from motorway. Wind downhill and pass under railway bridge. Turn immediately R, passing **Rolle** station (17km, 391m) (accommodation, refreshments, camping, tourist office, station).

Turn L at T-junction and R at roundabout. Continue to mini-roundabout and turn R under railway and L opposite Hammel winery. Where road bends L, turn R and continue over motorway. ◄ Turn L opposite industrial estate onto concrete track. Where this ends, turn R then L to continue through fields. Pass garden centre and turn R at T-junction. After 150m reach summit of climb and turn sharply L on cycle track along edge of woods. Pass under motorway then fork R at junction of tracks. Pass **La Côte** motorway service area R, then at end of buildings turn L to continue between fields. Dog-leg L and R over offset crossroads, continuing between fields, then follow track bearing L and R alongside woods. Turn L over stream and R to continue through fields. Go ahead over crossroads into **Gland** (26km, 431m) (accommodation, refreshments, station).

Go ahead over roundabout and leave village past aggregate quarry. ◄ Pass through Pont Farbel hamlet and turn L at crossroads. Cross railway bridge and turn R on track past airstrip. Continue beside railway, then after road bears L, turn R at crossroads and immediately L to continue beside railway into **Prangins** (29.5km, 418m) (accommodation, refreshments, station).

The **18th-century château** in Prangins (pop 4100), once the home of Voltaire and then later of Napoléon's brother Joseph, is now a museum dedicated to the history, culture, politics, economy and social life of francophone Switzerland.

The right turn is no-entry, but cyclists are permitted.

A line of concrete blocks crossing the road after the quarry is part of a Swiss Second World War defence line running from the Jura mountains to Lake Geneva, nicknamed 'Toblerones' due to their shape.

Continue through village, passing station R, and go ahead over roundabout. Turn R over railway bridge into beginning of **Nyon**, then L onto main road and pass under railway line. Cross Asse stream and continue to where road reaches large open square. ▶ Turn R (sp Nyon Gare), then continue ahead over roundabout and turn L to reach Nyon station R (32km, 405m) (accommodation, refreshments, tourist office, cycle shop, station).

To visit the centre of Nyon continue ahead past the square.

Continue beside railway and ahead over roundabout. Where road ends, continue ahead on track beside railway. Turn sharply R over railway then continue on cycle track, bearing gently L through woodland and on

NYON

Nyon (pop 21,700) is built on the site of Noviodunum, the first Roman settlement in Switzerland, established by Julius Caesar in 45BC. This grew into an important colonia with forum, basilica, baths and amphitheatre. A 10km-long aqueduct provided water,

Nyon castle overlooks Lake Geneva

while a sewerage system carried waste to the lake. It was captured by the Alemanni (AD259) who destroyed many of the buildings. Built on the site of the Roman city, medieval Nyon dates from the 11th century, with a castle that was added in the 12th century. In the early 14th century Louis I of Savoy established his court in the town and built a mint. During the Bernese occupation (1536–1798), Nyon became the regional capital and gained many new buildings. The lower town beside the lake developed as a commercial area with trade between France and Italy flowing through Nyon. Modern-day Nyon is well-known by football supporters as the headquarters of UEFA, European football's governing body. Draws for the Champions' League are broadcast across Europe.

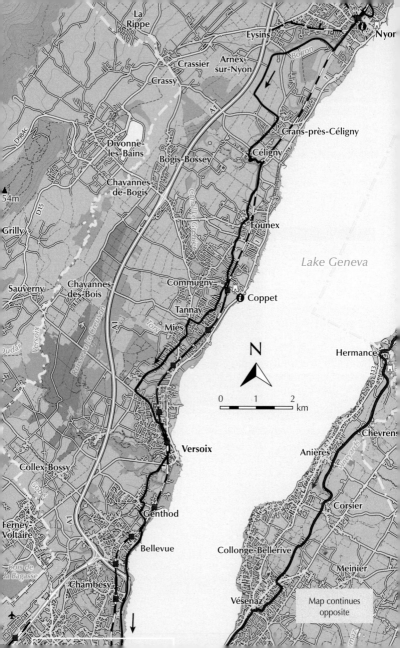

La Rippe

Eysins

Nyon

Crassier

Arnex-
sur-Nyon

Crassy

Crans-près-Céligny

Céligny

Divonne-
les-Bains

Bogis-Bossey

Chavannes-
de-Bogis

54m

Grilly

Founex

Lake Geneva

Sauverny

Chavannes-
des-Bois

Commugny

Coppet

Tannay

Hermance

Mies

N

Collex-Bossy

Versoix

Aniéres

Chevrens

Ferney-
Voltaire

Corsier

Genthod

Bois de
la bagasse

Bellevue

Collonge-Bellerive

Meinier

Chambésy

Vésenaz

Map continues
opposite

0   1   2 km

between fields. Cross a road and continue, bearing L, to crossing of tracks. Turn L to reach **Crans-près-Céligny** (37km, 426m) (refreshments).

Turn R at crossroads and continue through open country to reach **Céligny** (refreshments). Follow road winding downhill through village. Turn R, passing closed station L, and continue beside railway. Turn R at T-junction into **Founex** (accommodation, refreshments). Cycle through village and at end fork L. Continue past collège Terre-Sainte R to reach crossroads with **Coppet** station L (42.5km, 395m). ▶

Turn left to visit Coppet (accommodation, refreshments, tourist office, station).

> **Coppet** (pop 3250) is an attractive lakeside village with arcaded houses and a pink 18th-century château with literary connections. Originally the home of Jacques Necker, finance minister in Louis XVI's French pre-revolutionary government, it passed to his daughter Germaine de Staël, a novelist, playwright and essayist. Visitors to the house included Lord Byron in 1816.

Go ahead, then turn R at next crossroads with tree in middle of road. Turn R at T-junction to reach small roundabout in **Tannay** (accommodation, refreshments, camping, station).

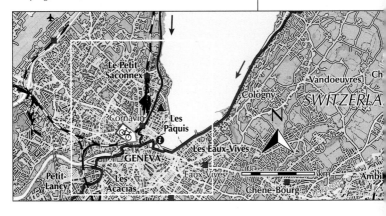

Turn R, then go ahead over painted roundabout and L at next roundabout. Follow road into **Mies** (accommodation, refreshments, station), and bear R through village. At end of village fork R (sp Collex) then continue past Versoix sports centre and turn L at roundabout. Continue through Pont-Ceard and cross railway bridge. Turn immediately L and L back under bridge parallel with railway R and continue to reach **Versoix** station R (49km, 388m) (accommodation, refreshments, station). ◀

Road is one-way with a contra-flow cycle lane.

Continue parallel with railway. At T-junction, continue ahead on cycle track between railway R and industrial building L. ◀ After 100m, turn R under bridge and L along other side of railway. Dog-leg L and R over Versoix stream on cycle track that runs below railway. At junction of tracks under viaduct keep R then bear L uphill. Go ahead over crossroads into open country. Turn L at crossroads in **Genthod** (station), then turn R opposite church. Continue past château, then turn L downhill. Bear R beside railway, then turn L under railway to reach roundabout on lakeshore. Turn R on cycle track beside main road and follow this through **Bellevue** (52.5km, 377m) (accommodation, refreshments, station).

To visit the centre of Versoix, turn left at the T-junction.

Follow cycle track bearing R under slip road of motorway junction. Continue past next road junction, then re-join main road and continue past Geneva zoo and botanical gardens R and headquarters of World Trade Organisation (WTO) L. ◀ At next major road junction, go ahead into street with tram tracks down centre to reach Pl de Cornavin. Continue past Geneva Cornavin station R, then go ahead over first crossroads and turn L behind Notre-Dame church. At next crossroads turn second R (first R is no entry), then where tram tracks bear L, continue ahead. Turn L downhill to reach Pl de St Gervais in centre of **Geneva** (58km, 374m) (accommodation, refreshments, YH, tourist office, cycle shop, station). ◀

To visit the Palais des Nations, former League of Nations headquarters, turn right onto Ave de la Paix opposite the WTO building.

For description of Geneva see end of Stage 6.

STAGE 5
St Gingolph to Thonon-les-Bains

Start	St Gingolph boat pier (384m)
Finish	Thonon-les-Bains, Port de Rives (381m)
Distance	28.5km
Waymarking	ViaRhôna EV17

This stage initially follows the shore of Lake Geneva from the French border to the up-market spa resort of Évian. It then climbs slightly above the lake to avoid busy main roads before descending to Thonon, the chief town of the Chablais district.

From Lake Geneva boat service pier in **St Gingolph**, follow Rue du Port NW beside lake. Pass Bellevue restaurant and turn R onto ramp leading to combined cyclist/pedestrian bridge over Morge stream. ▶ After bridge,

Morge stream is the Swiss/French border. It is unmanned and unmarked.

The fleet of paddle steamers on Lake Geneva are over 100 years old

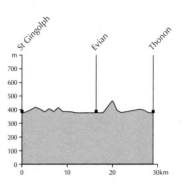

continue ahead beside lakeside promenade (Quai André Chevallay) to reach main road. Turn R using cycle track L then, opposite sign showing end of St Gingolph, turn L uphill under bridge and R on cycle track parallel with disused railway. Continue winding and undulating through

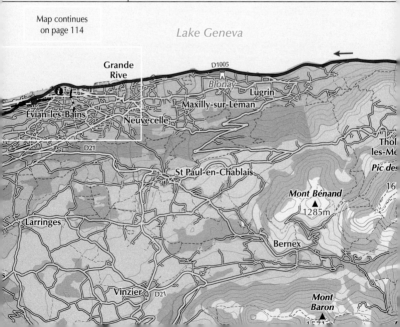

Map continues
on page 114

STAGE 5 – ST GINGOLPH TO THONON-LES-BAINS

woods past Chéniaz quarry L and through **Bret** (accommodation). Pass under railway to reach end of cycle track and turn L on D1005 main road through **Locum**, then continue through **Meillerie** (6.5km, 399m) (accommodation, refreshments).

Pass below centre of **Lugrin** (12km, 380m) (refreshments, camping) and go ahead through Tourronde. Continue through Torrent and **Grande Rive** (accommodation, refreshments) passing Port de Plaisance marina R and fork R at roundabout to reach landing stage for Lake Geneva boat services in **Évian-les-Bains** (16.5km, 382m) (accommodation, refreshments, gîte, tourist office, station).

Continue along lakeside promenade (Quai Baron de Blonay, D1005) and ahead uphill at roundabout (Ave Général Dupas). At next roundabout fork L (second exit, Rte de Bissinges, D11, sp Publier) uphill. Cross railway bridge and continue uphill into Ave des Rives du Léman. Turn R (Rue de la Flogère, sp Amphion) winding

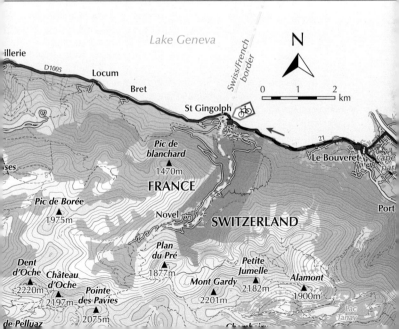

ÉVIAN

Évian (pop 9100) is known for mineral water in two guises: high-quality bottled water marketed worldwide and thermal baths fed by mineral water that are the central attraction of an up-market spa town. Legend has it that Evian water was first discovered in 1789 when the Marquis de Lessert, while out walking, drank from the Ste Catherine spring on the land of a monsieur Cachat.

The Cachat spring is the original Evian source

Lessert was suffering from kidney and liver problems and it appeared the water improved his health. Local doctors started prescribing the water and in response to this success Cachat fenced off his spring and began selling the water. Bottling began in 1826 and in 1859 a limited company was established to produce and market the product. Business grew steadily and in 1908 a close relationship began with glass bottle manufacturer Souchon Neuvesel (which became BSN). This eventually led, in 1970, to BSN taking full control of Évian and making it part of its Danone subsidiary. Evian water is still bottled locally in Amphion-les-Bains.

The first thermal baths date from 1824, eventually becoming part of the Hôtel des Bains. Other baths fed by mineral water were developed and by 1900 there were over 20 luxury hotels, a casino, theatre and funicular. The art nouveau pump room and baths opened in 1903 and the luxurious Royal Hotel was built in 1909. Évian attracted socialites and royalty, including British King George V and King Farouk of Egypt, and has maintained its status as a high-class resort. Post-war it became the favourite holiday destination for French president François Mitterrand.

In addition to the pump room and Cachat spring, other notable buildings include the villa Lumière (now the town hall) and palais Lumière (once a thermal spa, now a conference and cultural centre). The town centre is ringed by public gardens and various floral displays are created every summer.

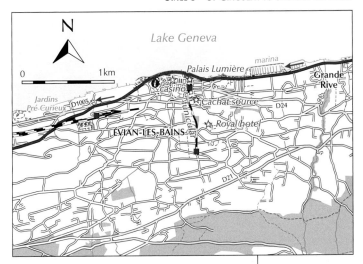

downhill. Cross railway and continue downhill into Rue de la Gare, becoming Rue de la Source. Bear R (sp village portuaire) then turn half-R (Rue du Clos Fleuri) at five-way junction, passing 'U' supermarket R. Go ahead (Rue du Port) across main road in **Amphion-les-Bains** (21.5km, 380m) (accommodation, refreshments, camping, tourist office).

Where road reaches lakeshore, turn sharply L (Rue de la Garenne). Go ahead over crossroads (Rte du Vieux Mottay) using cycle lane R and follow this ahead onto main road. Pass car park for Cite de l'Eau centre R, then fork L (Rue des Huttins) (camping) to reach T-junction and turn L (Rue de la Plaine). Turn R at triangular junction (Rue des Gennevrilles) then L at roundabout (Rue de Cartheray, third exit, sp Thonon). At next roundabout take second exit (Rue des Vignes Rouges, sp with Evian Water logo) parallel with D1005 and continue ahead with railway L over another roundabout. Cross small railway crossing and pass entrance to Evian bottling plant R.

Cross another small railway, then dog-leg L and R over larger railway crossing and continue (Rte d'Evian)

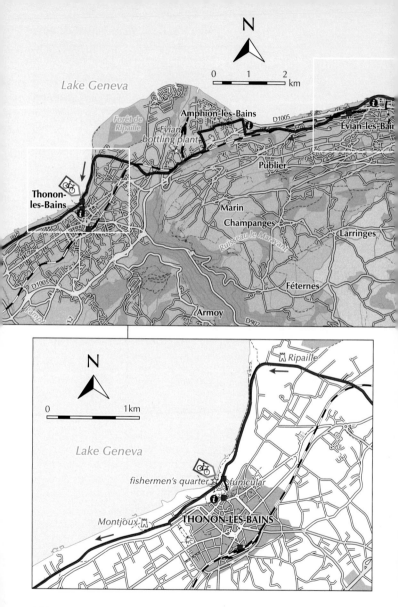

over river Dranse. Continue through Vongy (refreshments) and fork R (Ave de Ripaille, sp Port de Rives). Pass under railway bridge and go straight ahead over roundabout, joining cycle track R. Continue over next roundabout and follow road past Château de Ripaille R then bear L past Thonon plage bathing area and continue along lakeside promenade (Quai de Ripaille). Pass extensive marina R to reach road junction at Port de Rives (with funicular station L) in the fishermen's quarter below **Thonon-les-Bains** (28.5km, 381m) (accommodation, refreshments, camping, tourist office, cycle shop, station). ▶

Continue ahead onto Stage 6 or follow the road L steeply uphill to reach the town centre (alt 428m).

Thonon-les-Bains (pop 35,250), is the principal town of Chablais, a sub-département of Haute-Savoie, and the centre sits on a bluff 50m above Lake Geneva. From Port de Rives a funicular (which carries cycles) goes the short distance up to Ville Haute (upper town) where the historic centre can be found. The old Château de Sonnaz (1666), once home to one of Thonon's oldest families now houses the town museum and tourist office. Châteaux de Bellegarde had a defensive role as part of the fortifications. Thonon is *kilomètre zéro* (starting point) for various routes that head south through the highest parts of the French Alps to the Mediterranean coast, the most famous being long-distance path *grande randonnée cinq* (GR5) which runs for 660km from here to Nice.

STAGE 6
Thonon-les-Bains to Geneva

Start	Thonon-les-Bains, Port de Rives (381m)
Finish	Geneva, Pl de St Gervais (374m)
Distance	45.5km
Waymarking	ViaRhôna EV17 (France), Tour de Léman R46 (Switzerland)

The route undulates gently along the south shore of Lake Geneva. This stage keeps mostly a little way from the lakeshore, skirting a number of gated private developments before passing the floral lakeside villages of Yvoire and Nernier. After re-entering Switzerland at Hermance, a ride through suburban Geneva follows.

From Port de Rives, beside bottom funicular station in **Thonon-les-Bains**, follow Ave du Général Leclerc SW uphill. Where road turns sharply L, turn R (Ave de Corzent) downhill, using cycle track L. Pass entrance to Château de Montjoux R and continue downhill on

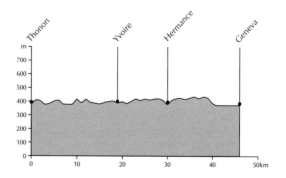

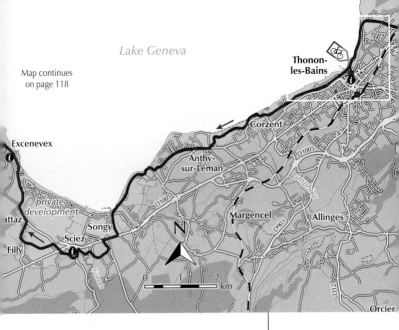

Map continues
on page 118

contra-flow cycle lane divided from traffic by wooden
bollards. Where one-way system ends in **Corzent**
(refreshments, cycle shop), continue downhill on road
then go ahead over mini-roundabout (Rue du Lac).
Follow this turning R and continue into Rue de la Plage
bearing L along lakeside. Bear R (Rue des Savoyances) at
roundabout and after 200m fork R (Rte des Rives). Follow
this street winding through area of private housing, eventually bearing L uphill, then turn R (Ch du Fresnay) to
reach T-junction. Turn L (Rue des Pêcheurs) and R at next
T-junction onto main road (Rue des Longettes, D33) into
Anthy-sur-Léman (5km, 401m) (accommodation, refreshments, cycle shop).

Fork R in front of parish church (Rue des Fontaines)
and continue out of village past cemetery R. Fork R (Rte
du Lavoret), winding through residential area. Pass campsite L (camping) and bear R (Rte de la Rovériaz). Turn R
at T-junction (Rte du Port de Séchex) and drop downhill
to Port de Séchex (accommodation, refreshments). Bear L

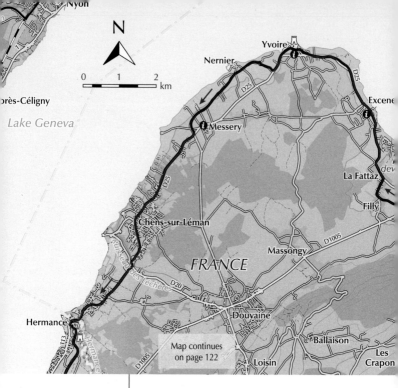

Between Songy and Excenevex the lakeshore is occupied by gated private residential developments requiring deviation away from the lake to circumnavigate these.

along lakeshore (Rte des Mouettes) and L again to reach roundabout. Turn R (Rte de la Renouillère), parallel with lakeside, to reach roundabout in **Songy** (9km, 374m) (refreshments, camping). ◀

Bear L (Rte du Port, sp Bonnatrait) uphill and turn R at T-junction (Ave de Bonnatrait, D1005). Follow main road into Bonnatrait (10km, 402m) (accommodation, refreshments) and turn L uphill beside building 611 (Rte de Perrignier, D35, sp Perrignier). Between Bonnatrait and La Fattaz, the route is waymarked with yellow provisional signposts, and may change. Turn R (Rte d'Excuvilly) first uphill then forking L downhill to T-junction. Turn L (Rte des Sénateurs), then pass house 98 and turn uphill steeply (Rte du Crêt Beule). Continue into Ave de l'Église and turn R immediately after church (Ch de la Rouette). Continue downhill past cemetery L and fork L at mini-roundabout to reach T-junction. Turn R and immediately L, then join cycle track R and go ahead over roundabout (second exit, sp Excenevex) in **Sciez** (12km, 399m) (refreshments, tourist office).

At second roundabout, turn R (Rte de Bordignin, third exit, sp Filly) and continue through **Filly**. At road junction in village, bear R (Ave du Crétoliers, D324) and continue to T-junction. Turn L (D25, sp Excenevex) to reach roundabout in **La Fattaz** hamlet. Bear R (Rte du Lac, D25, first exit), joining cycle track R and follow this past double roundabout at entrance to Excenevex beach to reach **Excenevex** (15.5km, 386m) (accommodation, refreshments, camping, tourist office).

Go ahead at roundabout (Rte d'Yvoire, becoming Rte d'Excenevex, sp Yvoire). After passing entrance to Château de Roverée R, join cycle track R and follow this winding through fields before returning to main road and following Rue des Bouchets past car parks R into **Yvoire** (19km, 388m) (accommodation, refreshments, camping, tourist office). ▶

To visit the medieval centre, bear right (Pl de la Mairie) through a stone archway.

Yvoire castle overlooks a pretty harbour

Yvoire (pop 1000) is a small but attractive medieval village on the tip of a peninsula at a narrow part of Lake Geneva. This position gave control of trade on the lake and led Count Amadeus V of Savoy to fortify the village and build a castle (1306). Captured by the Bernese in 1536, the castle was burnt and remained roofless for 350 years. During the 20th century the castle, ramparts, fortified gateways and many houses have been renovated and preserved and now make a much-visited tourist destination. Yvoire has developed a reputation as a floral village that first achieved top prize in the French national competition for best-kept village in 1959 with more awards following over the years. In 2002 the village represented France at European level and received the International Trophy for Landscape and Horticulture.

Pass entrance gateway and fork R (Rue des Terroz) past fortifications R, then bear L (Rue des Mollards) opposite second gateway and pass marina below R. Continue on cycle track beside Rte de Messery (D25) and follow this bearing R onto country lane (Ch de Fenéche). Turn L at T-junction (Ch du Moulin) then go ahead at crossroads (Ch de Perreuse). At next T-junction turn R onto roundabout and leave by second exit (Rte de Messery). ◀ Continue on Ch de Sergyieu, passing through edge of **Messery** (23km, 419m) (accommodation, refreshments, camping, tourist office). Go ahead (Rte de Belossy) at staggered crossroads. ◀

To visit Nernier (accommodation, refreshments), another attractive lakeside floral village, take the first exit from the roundabout.

To visit Messery turn left at roundabout.

Continue to larger roundabout and turn R onto main road (Rte des Repingons, D25) on cycle track L. Descend through Messery forest and continue on Rue du Léman, with views R across Lake Geneva to Jura mountains north of lake, to reach **Chens-sur-Léman** (26.5km, 417m) (refreshments, camping).

Bear L in village, continuing on Rue du Léman, now on cycle track R, going ahead over first roundabout to reach second roundabout. Bear L (Rte du Lac, third exit) and after 75m turn R (Rte d'Hermance, D25) on cycle track R. Follow road through Chens-le-Pont (refreshments) and cross Franco/Swiss border to reach **Hermance** (30km, 375m) (accommodation, refreshments, camping).

> **Hermance** (pop 1050) has been a border town since the border between France and Switzerland was defined at the end of the Napoleonic Wars in 1816. Established in the 13th century by the bishop of Geneva as a fortified town with a castle, it changed hands a number of times between Genevois, Bernese, Savoyard and French control. The castle was built in 1247 and, along with much of the village, was destroyed in 1589 during a war between Berne and Savoy; only the tower remained. The town remained an isolated backwater until a road was opened along the south side of Lake Geneva (1851) and steamship services started (1873). Before 1950 residents were mostly involved in agriculture, fishing or craft industries; nowadays the majority are employed in the service sector and commute to Geneva.

Continue through village with streets of old fishermen's houses R and remains of fortified tower on ridge L. At crossroads just before bus-turning circle, turn L uphill (Ch du Crêt-de-la-Tour) passing church behind cemetery wall L. Bear R (still Ch du Crêt-de-la-Tour) with tower of old castle L and continue uphill into Rte de Chevrens. At end of village follow road forking L into open country and through wine-producing village of **Chevrens**.

Continue through vineyards, then where road turns R continue ahead through Bassy and go ahead at roundabout onto Rte de la Côte-d'Or. Follow road winding through vineyards to reach T-junction. Turn R (Ch des Gravannes) and after 60m turn L (Ch du Pré-Puits) to go through **Corsier** (35.5km, 433m).

Continue on Ch des Bûchilles, becoming Ch de la Gentille, to reach St Maurice. Turn R at T-junction and after 50m L into Ch du Petray. Continue through open country to reach beginning of Vésenaz. ▶ At roundabout bear L (third exit) uphill into Ch des Tattes. After 250m, turn R (Ch de la Californie) through residential area and

From Vésenaz the built-up urban area is continuous to Geneva.

121

continue over crossroads into Ch de Trémessaz. Follow road downhill past cemetery R and round bends R and L. Turn R at T-junction (Ch des Rayes) into centre of **Vésenaz** (39km, 421m) (refreshments, camping).

Turn L at next T-junction (Ch du Vieux-Vésenaz) and continue onto Ch de la Haute-Belotte. Turn R at crossroads into Ch de Bonnevaux and continue over mini-roundabout downhill on Ch de Nant-d'Argent. Turn L at main road and continue on Quai de Cologny (cycle track R) with Lake Geneva R, passing **Cologny**. Pass Parc la Grange L and Port-Noir marina R, continuing ahead along lakeside on cycle track beside Quai Gustave-Ador into Geneva suburb of **Les Eaux-Vives** (accommodation, refreshments, cycle shop, station).

Pass **jet d'eau** (water jet) R and permanently moored paddle boat 'Genève' (now a restaurant), then bear R at T-junction on cycle track through edge of Jardin Anglais park. Opposite Geneva floral clock L, turn L across road using traffic lights and R on other side beside Quai du Général-Guisan, which soon becomes one-way with

Geneva's floral clock reflects the city's important watch-making industry

contra-flow cycle lane R. Where this ends, re-join road and continue ahead to reach Pl du Rhône. Turn R on Pont des Bergues) bridge across Rhone, passing Ile Rousseau R. Turn L (Quai des Bergues) and continue beside river to end of stage at Pl de St Gervais in centre of **Geneva** (45.5km, 374m) (accommodation, refreshments, YH, tourist office, cycle shop, station).

GENEVA

Geneva (pop 204,000 city, 519,000 metro) is one of the world's most international and cosmopolitan cities. For five centuries (1032–1530) it was a city state within the Holy Roman Empire. After gaining independence Geneva became a Protestant city, strongly influenced by the teaching of French theologian Jean Calvin who lived here from 1541–1564. Many Huguenot (French Protestant) families moved to the city to escape persecution in France, bringing with them skills in watch-making and banking, two of Geneva's principal industries. Briefly part of France under Napoléon (1798–1813), the city joined the Swiss Federation in 1814. It is nowadays Switzerland's second largest city although immigration, particularly from France, has re-established a Catholic majority.

The water jet at Geneva shoots water 140m in the air

Geneva's position as an international city began with the Geneva Convention (1864), which established the Red Cross and set out a code of conduct for treating victims of war. After the First World War the League of Nations was established here in the Palais des Nations, followed in 1946 by the European headquarters of its successor, the United Nations. Many other trans-national bodies have followed including the International Labour Organisation, the World Health Organisation and the World Trade Organisation. Most of them are grouped together in a series of office buildings just north of Lake Geneva. These international bodies, together with banks and European offices of some major companies, have contributed to 48 per cent of residents being foreign nationals.

The heart of the city is the old town, south of the Rhone. Principal sights include St Pierre cathedral (built 1160–1289), which is quite austere as most of its interior decoration was removed during the Protestant reformation. Nearby is the Auditoire Calvin where Calvin and Scottish Presbyterian reformer John Knox both preached. Other buildings include the town hall and the Alabama chamber where the Geneva Convention was signed. South of the old town in Bastion Park is the Reformation wall, a 100m-long monument featuring key figures in the establishment of European Protestantism, including Calvin, Knox and Oliver Cromwell. The view from the lakefront is dominated by the *jet d'eau*, a 140m-high water jet which is illuminated at night.

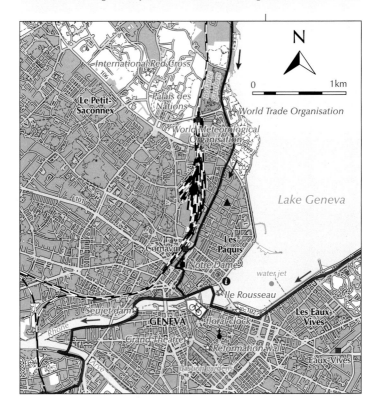

125

STAGE 7
Geneva to Seyssel

Start	Geneva, Pl de St Gervais (374m)
Finish	Seyssel, Pl de l'Orme (258m)
Distance	59km
Waymarking	Rhone route R1 (Switzerland), ViaRhôna EV17 (France)

The first 10km are taken up getting out of Geneva and its suburbs before continuing on through vineyards and verdant fields to the western tip of Switzerland. The route then climbs to cross the French border and follows the Rhone through the Défilé de l'Écluse gorge below the Vuache ridge. Another climb follows before a long descent to Seyssel. No towns are passed on this stage and once Geneva is left behind there is no accommodation until Seyssel.

Seujet dam controls the level of water in Lake Geneva.

From Pl de St Gervais in centre of **Geneva**, follow Quai Turrettini W alongside Rhone. Pass under first bridge then continue along Quai du Seujet and turn L on Passerelle du Seujet to cross river over Seujet dam. ◄

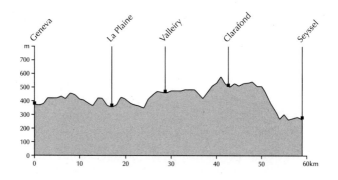

126

Pass between buildings and turn R (Rue de la Coulouvrenière). Continue along riverbank and pass under next bridge onto Sentier des Saules. Pass back of trolleybus depot L and where road narrows, turn L (Rue de la Truite). Continue over river Arve on Passerelle du Bois-de-la-Bâtie. At end of bridge follow gravel track R beside river and turn L (Rte des Péniches) back past bridge with Bois-de-la-Bâtie woods R. At next bridge turn R and after 30m bear R through barriers on cycle track steeply uphill beside Rte de Chancy. After 250m turn second R on winding cycle track ascending through woods with deep gulley L. At end, turn L across road and continue into Ch de Claire-Vue. Bear R (still Ch de Clair-Vue) and continue into Ch des Maisonnettes. Turn L at roundabout (Ave du Petit-Lancy) and L at end (Ave Louis-Bertrand). Cross road with tram tracks into **Lancy** (accommodation, refreshments, station).

Turn next R (Ch des Pâquerettes) then second L (Ch du Gué) and R again between first and second apartment

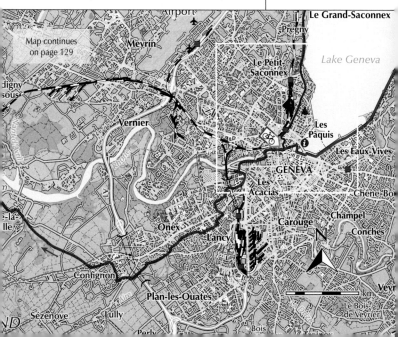

Map continues on page 129

buildings. Continue on cycle track over motorway bridge and ahead onto Vieux Ch d'Onex. Pass Collège De Saussure L and continue ahead on road to reach T-junction. Turn R and bear L to continue on Vieux Ch d'Onex. Continue over crossroads into Ch des Laz. Turn R at T-junction (Ch Charles-Borgeaud) and go ahead at roundabout in **Onex** (5.5km, 430m) (accommodation, refreshments).

Continue into Ch David-Brolliet, bending L and R. Cycle through barriers and cross main road to follow Ch de Sur-le-Beau with fields appearing L. Road becomes Ch de Narly and after 700m, where fields end, turn L (Ch de Murcie). Then follow road bearing R to emerge on Ch des Marais. Turn R to reach T-junction. Turn R steeply uphill (Ch de Mourlaz) to reach traffic lights in **Confignon** (accommodation, refreshments).

Turn R and immediately sharply L (Ch Pontverre), climbing past parish church R into village square. Bear L at fork, then R at crossroads (Ch de Vuillonnex). Continue over next crossroads into Rte de Pré-Marais and fork L (Ch de la Distillerie) to reach roundabout in Bernex (8.5km, 444m) (refreshments).

At roundabout, take first exit and fork immediately L (Ch de Saule). Turn R beside Peugeot garage (Ch de Paris) and cross main road, finally leaving built-up area of Geneva, and continue on cycle track descending through fields. Pass allotments R, continuing for 2km to reach road junction. Turn L, then immediately bear R at roundabout following Rue du Vieux-Four into **Aire-la-Ville** (12km, 379m) (refreshments, camping at Satigny 2km).

Turn L in village (Ch Moulin de Vert) and R at mini-roundabout (Ch des Crêtes). Continue through fields then turn L at T-junction onto road with cycle track L. ◀ Pass electricity-generating waste incinerator R and continue across Rhone over **Verbois** dam. Follow road ahead crossing railway bridge and winding uphill through vineyards. Turn L at T-junction (Rte de Mandement) and follow road winding through **Russin** (15km, 420m) (refreshments, station).

The wooden cross on the right commemorates a battle (1755) between villagers of Aire-la-Ville and those of the next village, Russin.

St-Jean-de-Gonville

Feigères

Péron

D884

Roulave

Dardagny

Verbois dam

Rhône

Russin

Aire-la-Ville

La Plaine

Challex

Avully

Cartigny

Épeisses

Gennecy

SWITZERLAND

Sez

Chancy

Avusy

Athenaz

Laconnex

Pougny

Sézegnin

Soral

D984b

Rhône

FRANCE

La Joux

Barre

Viry

D1206

Chevrier

A40

D1206

Valleiry

D1206

Vulbens

Faramaz

Chênex

Dingy-en-Vuache

A40

Bloux

Bois des Reynaud

Maisonneuve

Vers

D892

Murcier

Epagny

Jonzier

Savigny

Mont

N

0   1   2 km

Map continues on page 133

Drop down to cross river Allondon, then fork L (Rte de la Plaine) and cycle through hamlet of Le Moulin. Pass under railway bridge and bear R past Firmenich chemical factory L into **La Plaine** (17.5km, 354m) (refreshments, station).

Turn L at crossroads and leave village on bridge over Rhone. Ascend round hairpin bend to reach roundabout. Turn R (Rte d'Avully) and continue ascending into **Avully** (19km, 425m) (refreshments). Turn R at crossroads (Rte du Moulin Roget) and just past end of village fork R at roundabout (Rte d'Épeisses). Pass **Gennecy** and follow road descending past **Épeisses** R with Rhone in gorge below and France opposite. ◀ At Le Martinet hamlet, turn R and after 75m L (Ch de Couchefatte) over small bridge across stream. Turn R at T-junction (with turbine sculpture R) and R again at second T-junction on cycle track beside main road (Rte de Chancy, route 103), then continue into **Chancy** (23km, 364m) (refreshments, station).

Go ahead at mini-roundabout (Rte de Valleiry) following road curving L out of village and follow winding road ascending through woodland to reach Swiss/ French border (25.5km, 428m) at small clearing in trees. Continue ascending into open country (Rte de Chancy, D23) passing old French customs post R to pass through **La Joux**. At end of village, turn L uphill (Rte de Grateloup). Road winds gently uphill past stables L and market gardens to reach roundabout in **Valleiry** (28.5km, 464m) (refreshments, station). ◀

Go ahead (Rue du Pré Rosset) and continue ahead at second roundabout, taking third exit, then bear L (Rue de la Vosognette). Turn R beside railway (do not cross level crossing) into open country. At T-junction turn L over level crossing and immediately R on cycle track on opposite side. Follow this bearing L away from railway and continue through fields. Cross stream and turn sharply R. Bear R to emerge onto road and turn L into **Faramaz**. Turn R at mini-roundabout and fork R out of village. Pass small sports ground R, then turn R and zigzag over stream. Pass behind new houses to reach road (Rte du Carroz) and

Do not turn right into the village.

To reach the centre of town, turn left at the roundabout.

turn L on cycle track L. Go ahead past two roundabouts in **Vulbens** (32.5km, 484m) (refreshments).

At third roundabout turn R (Rue François Buloz, D908A) opposite town hall. Pass church R and go ahead over roundabout onto Rte de Chevrier, out of village. Pass through **Chevrier** (on Rue de Vulbens) and continue on Rte de la Semine. High wooded limestone ridge of Vuache mountain now dominates view ahead. Route follows road as it circles anti-clockwise around N end of ridge, cut into hillside passing between mountain L and Rhone in Défilé de l'Écluse gorge below R. Pass lookout point R with views towards Jura, then view down R to fort l'Écluse and **Longeray** railway viaduct crossing river. Descend past area L where landslip has swept away the trees leaving bare limestone, then ascend again past quarry L. Emerge from forest and pass below Arcine castle L to reach **Arcine** (40.5km, 547m).

The **Vuache** is a 10km-long thickly wooded mountain ridge (highest point 1101m) that marks the western border of French Genevois. Composed mostly of Jurassic limestone, it is an outlier of the

Fort l'Écluse can be seen in l'Écluse gorge below the Vuache ridge

Jura mountain range from which it is divided by the deep Défilé de l'Écluse gorge through which the Rhone starts forcing its way through the Jura. The western slopes form a sliding plane where the geological layers are tilted to such an extent that later layers slide down causing frequent landslips. French A40 motorway, the Autoroute Blanche that runs from Mâcon to Italy via the Mont Blanc tunnel, passes under the ridge by means of the Vuache tunnel.

Continue ascending past village (Rte du Vuache, D908A) to reach summit (575m) after 1km, then descend (Rte de Crêt du Feu) to **Clarafond** (42.5km, 506m) (refreshments). Pass through village on main road, going ahead over two roundabouts, and ascend into open country. Cross A40 motorway and pass Parc de la Croisée industrial estate R. Go ahead over roundabout (refreshments) and continue (now D14) across wooded plateau curving L to pass through **Chêne-en-Semine** (47km, 528m) (refreshments). Re-enter woods and turn L (Rte d'Usinens, D331, sp Usinens), descending gently. Fork R (Rte des Combay) then bear R at T-junction descending more steeply through open country to **Usinens** (51.5km, 415m).

Turn L in village and L again beside church (Rte du Pont Rouge). Beyond end of village, turn R downhill (Rte du Château de Châtel, D331, sp Seyssel). At bottom of hill, bear L past Châtel hamlet over river Usses and turn R onto main road (D992) using cycle lane R. Pass Seyssel dam R and continue beside Rhone. ◄ After 500m, follow cycle track forking R downhill towards river. Pass campsite L and bear slightly L onto Promenade F. Montanier and continue to reach Pl de l'Orme in centre of **Seyssel** (59km, 258m) (accommodation, refreshments, gîte, camping, tourist office, cycle shop, station).

Seyssel dam marks the limit of Rhone navigation, 260m above Mediterranean sea level.

Seyssel (pop 2300) straddles the Rhone with settlements in both Haute-Savoie (east bank) and Ain (west bank). For 100 years (1760–1860) the river

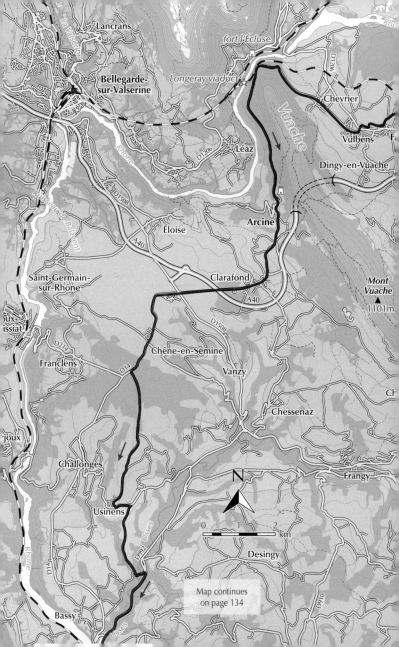

Lancrans

Île Valserine

fort l'Écluse

Longeray viaduct

D1206

Chevrier

Bellegarde-sur-Valserine

Vulbens

F

Rhône

D1206

Léaz

Vuache

Dingy-en-Vuache

D1508

Arcine

A40

Éloise

Clarafond

Saint-Germain-sur-Rhône

A40

Mont Vuache

▲ 1101m

D1508

ux-issiat

D214

Chêne-en-Semine

Franclens

D14

Vanzy

Chessenaz

Ch

joux

N

Challonges

Frangy

0   1   2 km

Usinens

Usses

D992

Desingy

D10

Map continues
on page 134

Bassy

Rhône

Usses

D14

The little town of Seyssel was a border town until 1860

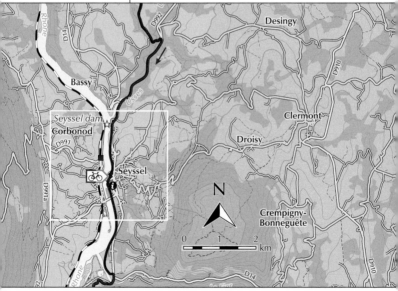

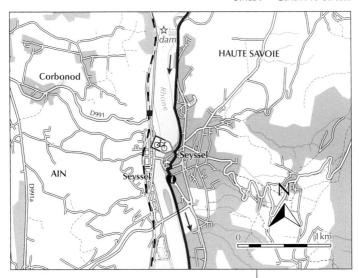

was an international border as Savoy was ruled by the Sardinians. The narrow chain bridge (built 1838) and nearby church feature in many pictures of the town. As the highest navigable point on the Rhone, before the railways came Seyssel was a busy port for goods being transhipped overland to Geneva. Local vineyards produce dry white and sweet dessert wines from altesse and molette grapes, which should be consumed young. A method-champenoise white sparkling wine is also produced. This is known as Royal Seyssel as the English Queen Victoria was known to have enjoyed this wine during her stays in Savoie.

STAGE 8
Seyssel to Champagneux dam

Start	Seyssel, Pl de l'Orme (258m)
Finish	Champagneux dam (211m)
Distance	53km
Waymarking	ViaRhôna EV17

The route continues southwest through a gap between the Jura and a series of outlying ridges east of the river, first following the Rhone through Chautagne and then the canal de Dérivation du Rhône west of the Parves ridge. This stage is mostly on the left bank and is generally flat, except for a small ascent to Châteaufort near the start.

Maison de haut Rhône is a cultural centre with exhibitions describing the life and history of the region.

From Pl de l'Orme in **Seyssel** cycle along Rue des Remparts, a small lane running SW downhill opposite post office from S corner of square. At end turn R (Rue de Savoie) and L (Rte d'Aix-les-Bains). Turn R on cycle track beside Maison de haut Rhône and L beside Rhone. ◄ Follow river under bridge and past sewerage works L. Emerge onto main road (Rte de Chautagne, D991) and turn R across river Fier. Continue ahead (cycle lane R) winding uphill into **Châteaufort** (4.5km, 294m) (accommodation, refreshments, cycle shop).

Follow main road (Rte des Allobroges) downhill and after 3km turn R (Rue de Stéphane Duc, sp Parc d'Activités de Motz-Serrières). Turn first L (Rte de Versières) to reach beginning of **Mathy** (8.5km, 245m) and turn R (Ch de la Digue Romaine). Pass old orchard L and turn sharply L then R between fields. Turn R at crossroads with car park ahead and continue winding through fields, then turn R and continue into woodland. Dog-leg R and L over stream then continue through woods passing beside Rhone R. Bear L away from river, then turn R.

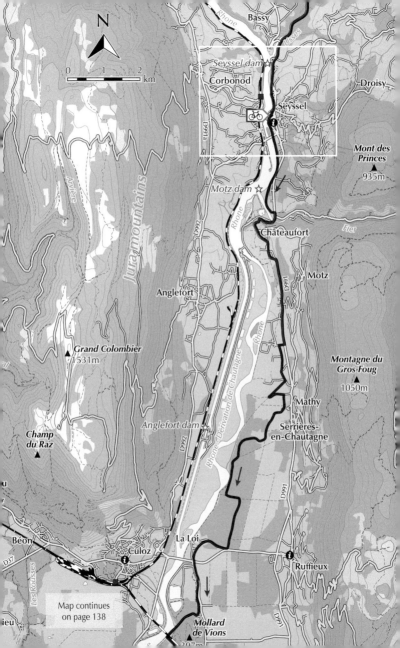

N

0 1 2 km

Rhone

Bassy

Seyssel dam ☆

Corbonod

Seyssel

Droisy

Mont des Princes
▲ 935m

Motz dam ☆

Rhone

Châteaufort

Motz

Arvière

Jura mountains

D992

Motz dam ☆

Fier

Grand Colombier
▲ 1531m

Anglefort

D991

Montagne du Gros Foug
▲ 1050m

Champ du Raz
▲

Anglefort dam ☆

Rhône–Dérivation de Chautagne

Rhone

Mathy

Serrières-en-Chautagne

D991

Béon

D37

Culoz

La Loi

Ruffieux

D991

Les Rousses

Map continues on page 138

▲ *Mollard de Vions*

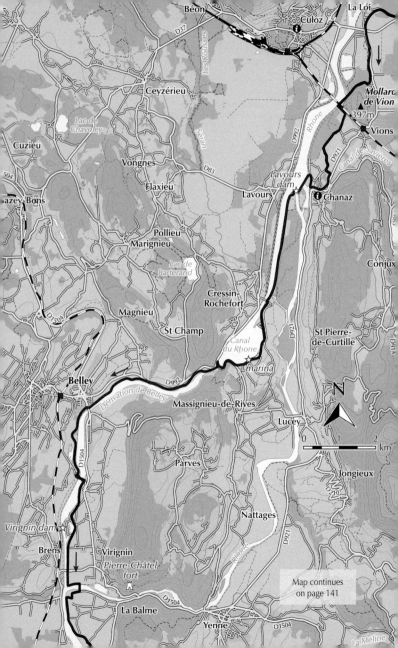

Map continues
on page 141

Turn R again then fork L (Rue Notre-Dame des Victoires) to pass **La Loi** R (16km, 239m) (refreshments).

At roundabout use barriers and crossing point to go clockwise around roundabout and continue ahead on cycle track L of road (sp Chanaz). ▶ After 350m cycle track switches to R then turns away from road and winds beside woodland to reach hamlet of Le Mollard. Turn R and continue to riverbank. Pass under railway bridge and turn immediately L (Rte de la Muraille) parallel with railway into La Muraille hamlet (refreshments). Turn R (Rte de la Digue Sarde) on cycle track into open country. ▶ After 500m fork R, then continue to T-junction. Turn L on cycle track beside road behind barriers R. Where barriers end, turn R on cycle track and continue to reach Canal de Savières then follow canal to reach pedestrian bridge opposite **Chanaz** (22.5km, 231m) (accommodation, refreshments, gîte, camping, tourist office).

To visit Culoz (refreshments, gîte, camping, tourist office, cycle shop, station) turn right at the roundabout and cross Rhone.

To visit Vions (accommodation, refreshments, station) continue ahead in La Muraille.

The canal de Savières connects the Rhone with Lake Bourget through Chanaz

Known as the little Venice of Savoy, **Chanaz** (pop 525) sits beside the Canal de Savières. This short canal connects the Rhone with Lac du Bourget, France's largest and deepest natural lake. In summer the canal is thronged with pleasure boats and the village is bedecked with flowers. Notable buildings include the old *moulin d'huile des noix et noisettes* (walnut and hazelnut oil mill). Built in 1868 and closed in the 1960s, this mill has now been restored to working condition.

Continue beside canal (do not cross bridge over canal) crossing entrance to marina. Bear R past campsite R and follow cycle track beside Canal du Rhône L. Pass roundabout and turn L over canal and lock. Cycle beside Rhone for 500m then turn R over **Lavours** dam. After dam, bear L passing hydroelectric station R then zigzag R and L onto asphalt cycle track beside flood dyke of canal de Dérivation du Rhône and follow this for 3km. Dog-leg R and L under Cressin-Rochefort bridge then continue beside canal. Cross road leading to Écoinçon (refreshments) then emerge onto road (Rte de Montaplan) and turn R passing La Tuilière hamlet L and campsite R. Where road turns L, bear R on cycle track continuing beside campsite to reach **Massignieu-de-Rives** marina (29km, 235m) (refreshments, camping, cycle shop).

To visit Belley (accommodation, refreshments, tourist office, cycle shop, station) turn right after the bridge and follow the road (D992) bearing left uphill into the town centre.

Pass alongside marina and turn R beside road (D37) on cycle track L. Pass through short tunnel and bear R onto road over canal into Ain département. Follow cycle track bearing R beside road (D992), then turn sharply R to drop down under bridge. Follow cycle track beside canal through gorge to pass under **Belley** bridge (34.5km, 232m) (refreshments). ◄

Dog-leg R and L to continue on cycle track following canal de Dérivation du Rhône. Turn L and R to pass under next bridge, then immediately R up to bridge and R across canal. Immediately after bridge turn R to reach waterside and bear L to continue on cycle track beside canal. Turn R at path junction and continue ahead on cycle track past **Port Virignin** marina and lock R. Pass

A new cyclists' suspension bridge links Virignin in Ain with La Balme in Savoie across the Vieux Rhône

under Virignin–Brens road bridge and follow track ahead beside canal, then bear L beside Vieux Rhône. Bear R to cross Vieux Rhône on new cycle bridge (40.5km, 224m).

FORT PIERRE-CHÂTEL CHARTREUSE

In the 13th century the Savoyards built a castle, nowadays called Fort Pierre-Châtel Chartreuse, on the slopes of the Parves ridge overlooking La Balme. This served to protect both the route through the gorge connecting Burgundy with Savoy's capital Chambéry, and the Rhone route to Geneva. In 1383 the castle was given to monks of the Carthusian order who adapted it into a chartreuse (charterhouse or monastery). However, because of its strategic importance the Dukes of Savoy maintained a military presence and the site became a fortified monastery. Although the castle changed hands several times between Savoy and France, the monastery thrived and grew until 1791 when the monks were forced to leave after all monastic houses in France were dissolved following the French Revolution. Used as a prison during the Napoleonic Wars, the site was developed after 1816 into a defensive fortress on the border between France and Sardinian controlled Savoy. However, French annexation of Savoy in 1860 made it redundant and it was downgraded to a support barracks. In 1926 it was auctioned off and bought by a private individual. It remains privately owned and cannot be visited.

On far side of bridge, turn R on quiet road and follow this bearing L, then turn R through woods to reach Rhone. Turn L beside river and continue with riparian woodland R and fields appearing L then bear R onto quiet road. Bear R at triangular junction then turn R on cycle track beside road with Rhone R, eventually bearing away from road but still following river. After 2km, zigzag L and R across drainage ditch. After another 2km, re-cross drainage ditch R and continue ahead to reach riverbank. Turn L and continue for 1km, with sheer limestone cliffs of Mont Tournier (877m) rising ahead, then turn L and R across drainage ditch for last time. Follow cycle track with drainage ditch R to junction of tracks just before **Leschaux** (51km, 214m).

Zigzag R and L onto flood dyke and continue past village, then zigzag L and R off flood dyke onto quiet road. Where this bears L, continue ahead on cycle track to reach end of stage beside **Champagneux** dam (53km, 211m). There are no facilities at Champagneux. ▸

To reach St Genix-sur-Guiers (5km off-route, 218m) (accommodation, refreshments, camping, tourist office) continue ahead (do not cross dam) then fork right following a signed cycle route along quiet country roads.

STAGE 9
Champagneux dam to Lagnieu

Start	Champagneux dam (211m)
Finish	Lagnieu, bridge (203m)
Distance	63km
Waymarking	ViaRhôna EV17

The route turns northwest at first following the Rhone below the Bugey ridge, the most southerly extension of the Jura mountains. It then crosses to the left bank and climbs gently away from the river before returning to the Rhone and following the Vallée Bleue to Lagnieu. This stage is mostly on quiet country roads and dedicated cycle tracks, with one gentle ascent (40m) but otherwise level.

Follow road (D125) W across **Champagneux** dam over original course of Rhone. After dam fork R on cycle track beside road. Pass Cuchet hamlet L and where road turns away L, continue ahead on cycle track along lakeshore. Opposite restaurant R (refreshments), turn L and R onto road (D992) and cross Rhone. After bridge, turn sharply R on cycle track then R again under bridge and continue beside river. Cross main road and ascend through barrier into **La Bruyère** (4km, 244m) (refreshments, camping).

Cycle ahead through centre of village (Rue de l'Espace Rhône, D19, sp Les Abrets) and continue over river bridge. Turn R on cycle track towards industrial estate then follow this bearing R to river and turn L along riverbank. Just before dam, bear L away from river, with boat portage road R, then turn R over **Brégnier-Cordon** dam. ◀

Turn L parallel with road and bear L to follow riverside cycle track for 3km. Pass under bridge and turn R uphill away from river on winding cycle track. Turn L beside road and after 40m L again (Rue du Pont) into **Évieu** (10.5km, 207m) (refreshments).

Although the Rhone is navigable downstream from Seyssel, there is no lock at Brégnier-Cordon. To pass this obstacle, boats are transported overland for over 600m in cradles along a dedicated portage road.

Map continues
on page 148

Colomieu

Arbignieu

Le Port de
Groslée

Groslée

Tours

D19

St Bois

angues

St Benoît

Prémeyzel

D33

La Sauge

hage

Évieu

Rhône

D10

Glandieu

Izieu

Brégnier-Cordon
dam

Brégnier

La Bruyère

Gélignieux

Murs

Les Avenières

Brégnier-Cordon deviation

Champagneux dam

Thuellin

Cordon

Rhône

Corbelin

N

Guiers

St-Genix-
sur-Guiers

Faverges-
le-la-Tour

Granieu

Aoste

At T-junction, turn L and fork immediately L (Rue du Château, sp La Sauge). Follow this out of village and bear R through forest to **La Sauge**. Turn L at T-junction (Rte de la Sauge), pass through hamlet and fork L on cycle track beside river. Bear R away from river through forest, then return to riverbank and emerge on riverside road. Bear L to reach **Le Port de Groslée** (16.5km, 208m).

Pass under bridge, then after 100m fork R away from river. Turn R at T-junction then R again (D198) over bridge across Rhone into Isère département. Immediately after bridge turn sharply R onto cycle track. Follow this bearing L through barrier and continue beside river. Turn L at first junction then R at T-junction in **Tours** (refreshments, camping) and follow winding road through open country. At second bend, where road bears R, continue ahead on cycle track through fields. Turn L at T-junction on quiet road winding through fields and woods. After 1km, turn R through barrier onto cycle track and bear R at path junction. Pass grave of Paul Claudel visible over wall L then bear L and continue to T-junction. Turn L (D60), to reach entrance to **Château de Brangues** L (21km, 218m). ◄

To visit Brangues (refreshments, camping) continue ahead for 500m.

> **Château de Brangues** was bought in 1927 by writer, poet and former diplomat Paul Claudel (1868–1955) who is buried in the surrounding park. It is still owned by his descendants.

Turn R and pass through small hamlet then turn R on cycle track between fields. Turn R at T-junction, then where asphalt ends turn sharply L on cycle track. Cross small stream and bear R to road junction. Turn L, then join cycle track R and follow this bearing R beside Rte de Marais (D60a). Turn R at crossroads (Ave Paul Claudel, sp Lycée) then L opposite car park on cycle track beside school. Emerge beside main road and bear R on cycle track to reach roundabout in **Morestel** (26.5km, 211m) (accommodation, refreshments, camping, tourist office, cycle shop).

Although **Morestel** (pop 4500) is nowadays a commuter town for Lyon, at its heart is an old medieval walled settlement that grew up around a 13th-century castle perched on a rocky outcrop. This was destroyed during the 16th-century religious wars, with only the central keep and dungeon remaining. The dungeon has been restored and is now an exhibition space and art gallery. Other sights include St Symphorien church with a Gothic tower that dominates the skyline, and Maison Ravier, the former home of French landscape artist François-Auguste Ravier (1814–1895).

Just before roundabout, cross road to L and follow cycle track 'wrong-way' around roundabout. Continue ahead (Ave du Pré du Roi, D1075, third exit, sp Bourg-en-Bresse) using cycle track L and follow this ahead over two more roundabouts. Where cycle track ends, fork L (Ch de la Plaine de Crévières) ascending gently through fields. Bear L at second crossing of tracks. Where cycle track ends, go ahead over crossroads (Rte de la Plaine) and after 80m, fork L (Ch de la Massotière) through **Crévières** (30.5km, 243m) (accommodation).

Go ahead over crossroads then bear R at T-junction (Ch du Bron) and fork L (Ch du Vert). Turn L at T-junction (Rte de Chassins) and after 200m, turn R on cycle track winding downhill through woods. Pass limestone quarry L then turn R (Ch de l'Épaud) at T-junction. Go ahead over crossroads in l'Épaux hamlet (refreshments) into Rte de Champolimard. Turn second R on cycle track along former railway trackbed. Pass Étang de Fongeau lake L and go under road bridge at site of old station in **Arandon**.

Emerge on road (Rue des Cités) and continue ahead between derelict aluminium smelter R and series of small lakes L. Where road bears R, fork L into forest on cycle track along old railway. Emerge on road (Rue du Devin) and turn R then bear L under limestone conveyor. ▶ Where trees end, turn L on cycle track through fields. At junction of cycle tracks, fork R into forest and continue on winding cycle track. After end

For next 6km, the old railway trackbed is occupied by a covered conveyor belt taking limestone from local quarries to Vicat cement works near Montalieu-Vercieu.

147

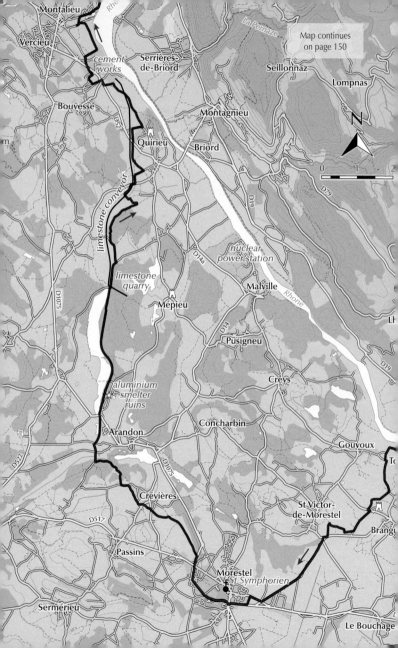

Montalieu

Vercieu

cement
works

Bouvesse

Serrières-
de-Briord

La Pernaze

Seillonnaz

Lompnas

Montagnieu

Quirieu

Briord

Map continues
on page 150

N

0   1   2

limestone conveyor

limestone
quarry

D1075

Mépieu

nuclear
power station

Malville

Rhone

D14a

D14

Pusigneu

Creys

aluminium
smelter
ruins

D522

Arandon

Concharbin

Gouvoux

To

D1075

Crévières

St Victor-
de-Morestel

Brangu

D517

Passins

Morestel
St Symphorien

Sermérieu

Le Bouchage

of trees, continue through fields for 200m then turn L towards another wood and continue winding beside forest with fields L and forest R. Cross conveyor and turn immediately R beside conveyor R. At crossroads, dog-leg R and L across conveyor to continue with conveyor now L. Opposite farm, turn R away from conveyor, then after 200m turn L through fields. Dog-leg L and R over conveyor and continue on cycle track winding through fields. At next crossroads, dog-leg R and L across conveyor and continue beside conveyor L. At next road crossing, turn R and follow road (Montée de Quirieu) uphill to beginning of **Quirieu** (43.5km, 236m).

Turn sharply L (Ch de St Roch) downhill and follow cycle track through fields. Cross conveyor for last time then bear L, passing large circular cement silos R, to reach T-junction. Turn R on cycle track R of road, then continue across two crossroads at entrance to Vicat cement works (45.5km, 219m). ▸

Turn L away from factory opposite works entrance on cycle track and follow this bearing R to reach road. Turn R then L (Rue du Stade) at mini-roundabout. Go ahead over next roundabout and follow cycle track to reach main road (D52). Turn L, using cycle track R, and

The cycle route follows a limestone conveyor belt for 6km

Louis Vicat discovered the properties of artificial cement in 1836 and the company he founded has grown to be one of the largest cement companies in the world.

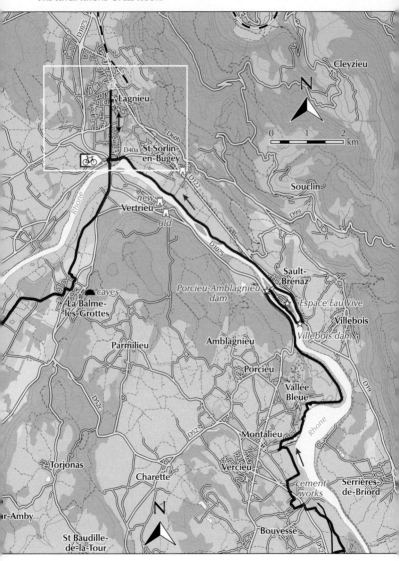

follow this forking R away from road. After 300m, turn R through fields and follow cycle track bearing L to reach T-junction. Turn L beside river Furon R, then turn sharply R onto bridge over river and continue to T-junction. Turn R (Rue du Rhône). After 250m, follow cycle track R away from road winding alongside le Gauchon lagoon R. Turn R on road and follow this bearing L beside Rhone R. Where road ends at turning circle, continue ahead on cycle track winding through Vallée Bleue leisure park in **Montalieu-Vercieu** (49.5km, 205m) (accommodation, refreshments, gîte, camping, tourist office, cycle shop).

After leisure park, pass marina R, and continue beside river for 4.5km to reach **Porcieu-Amblagnieu** hydroelectric dam. ▶ Turn R over dam onto Ile de la Serre and R again between dam R and disused lock L.

> On the Ile de la Serre is the **Espace Eau Vive**, a water park with facilities and courses for canoeing, kayaking and white-water rafting. The old lock on the island, which allowed boats to pass Villebois dam, is no longer operable and has been replaced with a portage ramp.

Narrow gauge railway beside cycle track L is the 4km-long chemin de fer de Haute Rhône from La Vallée Bleue to Sault-Brenaz. Trains run on Sundays and holidays only.

Old lavoir (wash-house) in Lagnieu

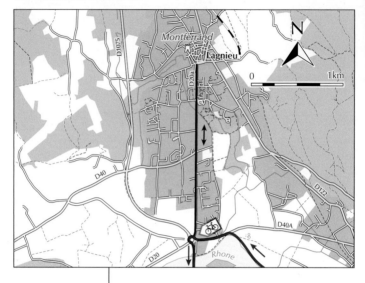

Cross portage ramp and pass **Espace Eau Vive** water park L, then bear L across **Villebois** dam over main stream of Rhone. Turn L and follow cycle track, now on Rhone's right bank, to **Sault-Brénaz** bridge (57km, 200m) (accommodation, refreshments, camping).

To reach the centre of Lagnieu, take the first exit from the roundabout and follow Rte du Port to the town centre.

Pass under bridge and continue on riverside cycle track for 5.5km, passing old and new châteaux in **Vertrieu** on opposite bank of river L, to reach main road (D40A) and turn L to reach roundabout on edge of **Lagnieu** (63km, 203m) (accommodation, refreshments, cycle shop). ◀

> **Lagnieu** (pop 7200) was an old walled town with 15th-century Château Montferrand at its north west corner. Although the walls have been dismantled, the narrow maze of streets inside the walls remain and are the site of a twice-weekly market. The main employer is a large St Gobain factory which produces glass and artificial diamonds.

STAGE 10

Lagnieu to Lyon

Start	Lagnieu, bridge (203m)
Finish	Lyon, pont de la Guillotière bridge (165m)
Distance	64.5km
Waymarking	ViaRhôna EV17. No waymarking between Les Cinq Chemins (23.5km) and Pommier (36.5km). This section is provisional and may change when a definitive route is waymarked.

Starting beneath the sheer limestone cliffs of the Balcon de la Rhône with its caves and karst lakes, the route soon reaches a flat plain that extends all the way to Lyon. Small villages give way to dormitory towns and later a continuously built-up conurbation. For half the distance the route is mostly on minor roads and dedicated cycle tracks, then after Jons voies vertes are followed along canal towpaths and through the Miribel-Jonage park all the way to the centre of Lyon. The stage is mostly level with two slight ascents.

From roundabout below **Lagnieu**, follow road (D1075) S over Rhone bridge and join cycle track R of road. At next road junction, fork R beside D65 and after 1km fork R on quiet road past farms. At beginning of **La-Balme-les-Grottes** (4km, 208m) (refreshments, camping), follow asphalt surface bearing L and winding through fields. Emerge beside main road and dog-leg R and L across side road. Pass large car park R and turn R at roundabout (Rte de Travers, D65H). ▶

> To visit the centre of La Balme, turn left at the roundabout.

> **La-Balme-les-Grottes** (pop 1075) sits below sheer limestone cliffs into which there is an extensive cave system. Inhabited by both animals and humans since Palaeolithic times, the caves have yielded many archaeological finds that are displayed in the museum in Hières-sur-Amby. The

caves have been open to visitors since 1807. Attractions include a chapel built into the entrance, many natural rock features, underground streams and pools, a 130m-long lake and a portrait of French king François I (1494–1547) who visited the caves. The interior is lit to emphasise the limestone formations and water features. Twenty species of bat inhabit the caves.

Bear L (sp Travers) at crossroads and follow road bearing R out of village, winding through fields. Pass **Travers** and continue to **La Brosse** (8.5km, 203m) (camping). Turn L in village (Ch de la Fontaine) then R at T-junction (Ch du Marais). At next T-junction, turn L out of village on quiet road ascending through fields. Where road ahead becomes unsurfaced, bear R and continue to emerge on D65H road. After 300m, join cycle track L of road, then follow this crossing to R and across side road. Continue across D65 main road, then turn R beside main road and L at T-junction (Ch du Port de la Bruine). Turn R (Rte de Marignieu) at next T-junction and R again (Ch de Stade) past campsite L. Bear L (Ch des Moines) then continue to T-junction on edge of Le Moulin d'Avaux and turn L (Rte des Usines, D52A) and follow road into **Hières-sur-Amby** (14km, 235m) (accommodation, refreshments, camping).

Hières-sur-Amby (pop 1150) is another village beneath sheer limestone cliffs, on top of which is the Larina plateau with an archaeological site that contains remains of successive settlements from the Bronze Age to the Middle Ages. Different parts of the site have been excavated to reveal Gallo-Roman, Burgundian and Merovingian buildings and a church surrounded by a large necropolis.

At offset crossroads by Café du Lac bear R ahead uphill (Montée de la Cure, D65C) and ahead (Pl de l'Église, sp Crémieu) opposite church. Follow road bearing L into Pl de la République then go ahead (Rue du Colombier). After end of village, fork R downhill with

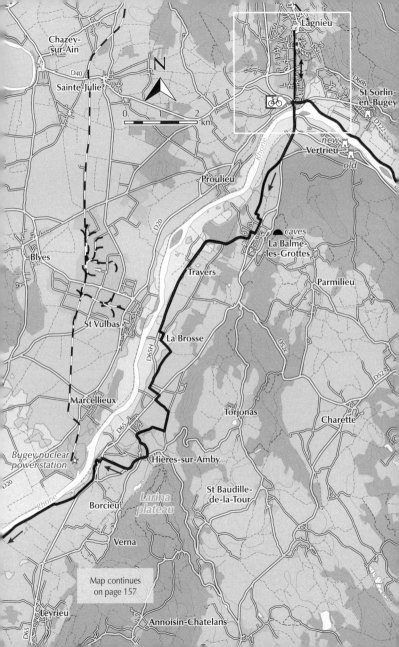

Chazey-
sur-Ain

Sainte-Julie

D40

Lagnieu

St Sorlin-
en-Bugey

D60b

D122

new
old

Vertrieu

Proulieu

Rhône

caves

La Balme-
les-Grottes

Parmilieu

Blyes

D20

Travers

St Vulbas

D65H

La Brosse

D52G

D52

Marcellieux

D65

Torjonas

Charette

Bugey nuclear
power station

Rhône

D20

Hières-sur-Amby

Borcieu

Larina
plateau

St Baudille-
de-la-Tour

Verna

Map continues
on page 157

Leyrieu

Annoisin-Chatelans

D65

N

0   1   2
═══════════════════ km

Bugey nuclear power station visible ahead and continue to reach T-junction in St Étienne (15km, 212m).

Turn L (Grande Rue de St Étienne, D65, sp Crémieu) then R beside house 22 (Rue du Vieux Puits). Turn L at T-junction (Rue des Balcons du Rhône) then fork R steeply downhill at triangular junction and bear L out of village. Where road comes parallel with main road, continue ahead on asphalt cycle track. Follow this for 5km, soon bearing away from main road through fields with Rhone R. Turn R at T-junction (Ch de Peillard) in Le Peillard hamlet (21km, 200m).

Pass pond L then follow road forking R and winding through fields. At beginning of **Le Port**, fork R (Ch du Port) to reach Rhone, then turn L and L again (Lotissement le Port) back through village. At end, turn R to reach roundabout and go straight ahead (Rte de Loyettes, D18, sp Chavanoz). Pass through residential development of **Les Cinq Chemins** (23.5km, 198m) (accommodation,

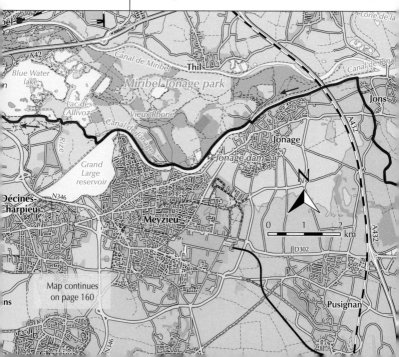

refreshments) and at next roundabout go ahead R (second exit, Rte de Belmont, sp Belmont). ▶ Pass car repair workshop R and join cycle track R. Cross river Bourbre and turn R (Rue du Moulinage) to reach staggered crossroads on edge of **Belmont**. Go ahead then immediately turn sharply R on cycle track above but parallel with D24A road. At T-junction in Le Bouchet hamlet, turn L on busy main road (Rte de Lyon, D55, sp Villette d'Anthon) uphill through edge of **Chavanoz** (refreshments). After village, turn second R (Ch de Revois, sp ZA Anthon) between fields past industrial area R to reach **Anthon** (28.5km, 208m).

From Les Cinq Chemins to Pommier the route is not waymarked.

Turn L at T-junction (Rte de Lyon, D55E), then dogleg L and R across main road onto rough track winding through woodland. ▶ Bear R under road bridge and pass **Club de Romagne** private housing development R. Turn L at crossroads (D124), then R (Rue des Fauvettes, sp Pusignan) at beginning of **Asnières** (refreshments).

The track can be muddy when wet.

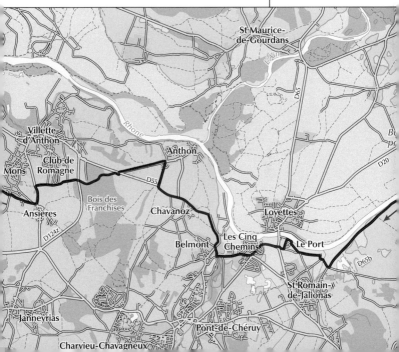

Turn L and R to continue ahead (Ch de Decrozo) at staggered crossroads in **Mons** (33.5km 220m), then continue on quiet country lane. After bend L and R, fork R (Ch de Pommier) winding through fields. Turn R at T-junction in hamlet of Pommier, then go ahead at roundabout (Ch des Meules) into **Jons** (37.5km, 204m) (accommodation, refreshments). Pass town hall L and join cycle track R of road. Follow this, bearing R at T-junction, and continue downhill to Jonage canal towpath.

Turn L along good quality gravel *chemin de contre-halage* (upstream towpath) then pass under motorway

This sign in Miribel-Jonage park is the first showing the distance to 'La Mer' (the sea)

and high-speed railway bridges and emerge beside river-side road to reach **Jonage** bridge (42km, 182m) (accommodation, refreshments). Turn R over bridge and L along opposite bank. Pass Jonage dam and pass under **Meyzieu** bridge (46.5km, 180m) (accommodation, refreshments).

> **Meyzieu** (pop 34,000) is part of the Greater Lyon metropolitan area. In 1960 it was a village of 2000 people, but the establishment of a large industrial estate in 1961 (which now covers over 300ha) and rapid expansion as a commuter suburb saw population grow to 25,000 by 1980. Northwest of the town, the Grand Large reservoir separates Meyzieu from the Miribel-Jonage park.

Continue along canal bank past Pont d'Herbens bridge (refreshments, camping), which crosses canal de Jonage at point where it opens into Grand Large reservoir. After 600m bear R off flood dyke then after another 100m turn R away from lake. ▶ Turn first L and fork R to follow asphalt cycle track winding through **Miribel-Jonage park**.

The signpost at the turn-off shows 'La Mer 368km', the first mention of the final destination of the ViaRhôna.

MIRIBEL-JONAGE PARK

The route passes through Miribel-Jonage park for 10km. In 1857 the Miribel canal (north of the Rhone) opened to aid river shipping and in 1899 the Jonage canal (south of the Rhone) was constructed to divert water over the Cusset hydroelectric dam. The land between them became a 28.5km^2 island with the winding course of the old Rhone flowing through it. This low-lying frequently flooded area was left untouched until 1968 when a project to reclaim the land commenced. This project had four aims: to create a recreational area, to provide drinking water for rapidly growing Lyon, to act as a floodplain containing excess river flow thus preventing floods downstream and to reclaim land for development. This last aim was later dropped and replaced with an objective to protect natural heritage. The main features of the park include the Grand Large reservoir on the Jonage canal above the Cusset dam and the Blue Water lakes for recreation and flood prevention on the course of the old Rhone. Around these features are areas of woodland and sporting facilities. The park attracts nearly four million visitors annually.

Continue beside Lac des Allivoz R, then cross road and pass car park L. Follow cycle track still winding through park, passing series of lakes R and eventually bearing L to emerge on track beside road L. Turn R to circle another car park with park admin buildings R (52km, 177m) and continue past golf driving range R. Pass between roundabout L and yet another car park R (refreshments). Just before road crosses causeway over course of old Rhone, turn L across road and continue on cycle track parallel with river (do not cross causeway). Pass under motorway bridge and bear L following cycle track beside service road. Where road turns L under motorway, continue ahead on cycle track beside motorway. Pass motorway junction L and continue between motorway L and canal R. Follow canal past aggregates depot L and turn L under pipe bridge. ◀ Emerge onto road Rue du Canal, using cycle track L, and just before

This is the point where canal de Jonage and old Rhone re-join.

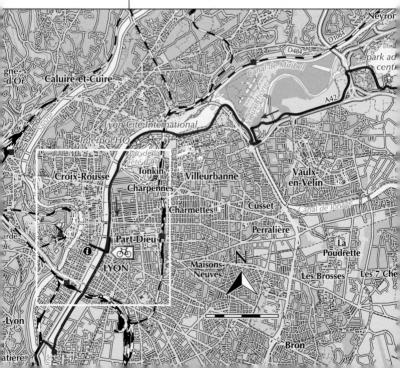

road overbridge, turn L then fork R uphill on cycle track and turn sharply R up ramp onto Croix Luizent bridge (57km, 172m).

Cross canal de Jonage and bear R to follow cycle track winding downhill. Turn L across two motorway slip roads and R and L onto gravel track alongside canal de Jonage. Follow cycle track beside canal R past water works L and under road bridge. At point where canal de Miribel re-joins Rhone, follow cycle track L under motorway bridge and continue through Feyssine park, now parallel with Rhone R. Cycle through woods and continue under Raymond Poincaré road and rail bridges (60.5km, 170m).

Continue along riverbank cycle path beside Quai General de Gaulle past **Lyon Cité International** L and under new combined cycle and footbridge over Rhone R. ▶ Continue on riverbank cycle track under six bridges and pass white façade of black-domed Grand

Lyon's Pl Bellecour is one of the largest city squares in France

Lyon Cité International is a new development of convention centre, hotels, offices and contemporary art museum. The last modern glass building, behind high security fences, is the world HQ of Interpol.

161

LYON

Lyon (pop 520,000 city, 1,670,000 metro) is France's second largest conurbation. The first settlement (Lugdunum) was founded (43BC) by the Romans on Fourvière hill, close to the confluence of rivers Rhone and Saône. It grew to become capital of Gaul and was the birthplace of two emperors, Claudius and Caracalla. After the fall of Rome, Lyon became capital of Burgundy (AD461), eventually becoming part of France in the 14th century. Positioned on the route between Paris and Italy, it developed as a major trade and financial centre. During the Industrial Revolution it became a centre for silk production, which led to further industrialisation and rapid growth.

The oldest part of the city (Vieux Lyon) can be found beside Fourvière hill, west of the Saône. On the hill (known locally as 'the hill that prays') are Notre-Dame basilica, the archbishops' palace, several convents and the Tour Métallique TV tower. Between the rivers, Croix-Rousse hill was the site of many small silk workshops, giving it the contrasting name 'the hill that works'. Presqu'île, the peninsula between Rhone and Saône, is the 18th-century heart of the city and the location of many grand buildings including those around Pl Bellecour, one of the largest city squares in France, and Rue de la République. East of the Rhone is Part-Dieu, the modern commercial centre with a number of tall office buildings while the flat plain further east is both a residential and industrial area. North of Part-Dieu are residential areas and the Tête d'Or park, which contains a zoo and botanic gardens overlooked by the new Cité International development.

Among Lyon's most notable residents, Auguste and Louis Lumière (the Lumière brothers) were pioneers of film and cinematography. Their first film, *Sortie de l'usine Lumière de Lyon* (1895), is considered the world's first motion picture, even though it lasts only 46 seconds. They later abandoned cinema believing it to be 'an invention with no future' and concentrated on developing colour photography. They launched the Autochrome Lumière colour photo process in 1907 and the company they founded grew to become a major producer of colour photographic products. Many of their inventions can be seen in the Musée Lumière, Auguste Lumière's former residence.

Lyon has a high concentration of restaurants per head of population and is often called the gastronomic capital of France, no mean accolade in a country renowned for its cuisine. This is partly due to the presence of a number of leading chefs, but also to its location between regions producing quality produce and fine wines, such as Burgundy (to the north) and Côtes du Rhône (to the south). Bouchons are small Lyonnaise restaurants specialising in local dishes at affordable prices originally aimed at the working population but nowadays much frequented by tourists and the French middle class.

Hôtel-Dieu, which occupies whole riverfront on opposite bank between sixth and seventh bridges, to reach stage end under pont de la Guillotière bridge in **Lyon** (64.5km, 165m) (accommodation, refreshments, youth hostel, camping, tourist office, cycle shop, station). ▶

To visit city centre, fork L after sixth bridge then turn R across Guillotière bridge and continue ahead to Pl Bellecour.

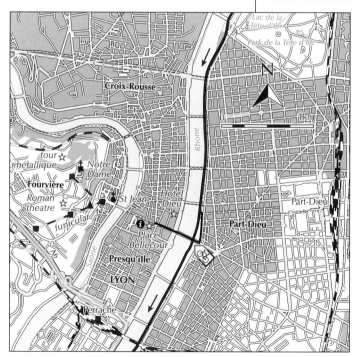

STAGE 11
Lyon to Vienne

Start	Lyon, pont de la Guillotière bridge (165m)
Finish	Vienne, Ste Colombe quayside (152m)
Distance	35.5km
Waymarking	ViaRhôna EV17 (inconsistent). Vernaison to Givors waymarked with yellow provisional signs

Below Lyon, the Rhone heads south through a broad valley all the way to the Mediterranean. After following the riverbank cycleway through Lyon, this stage follows roads out of the city west of the river, then crosses to the east bank to follow rough tracks alongside the Rhone Dérivation canal. A road alternative allows the rough section to be by-passed. Crossing back to the west bank, cycle tracks are used to reach Ste Colombe opposite the ancient Gaulish capital of Vienne. This stage is the least cycle friendly of all stages, and there is the option of taking a train from Lyon (Part-Dieu) to Vienne and restarting your ride with Stage 12.

From below pont de la Guillotière bridge in **Lyon**, follow riverside cycle track SW beside Rhone R past swimming pool complex with four white towers L. Pass under two road bridges and Perrache railway bridge then continue under two more bridges. After 75m, turn sharply L back up towards bridge approach and turn L on modern pont Raymond Barre combined tram and cycle bridge over Rhone. On opposite bank, pass ultra-modern building of **Musée des Confluences** L (3.5km, 168m) and go ahead under motorway bridge. Turn L beside motorway, using cycle lane R, and continue on pont de la Mulatière bridge over river Saône. At complicated road junction, follow cycle markings on carriageway taking you R of road via a series of crossings past mini-roundabout L, then re-cross road and bear R (sp Quai P Semard). Continue past Aquarium de Lyon R and pass confluence of Saône

Map continues
on page 168

Lyon's ultra-modern Musée des Confluences sits between the rivers Rhône and Saône

and Rhone beyond motorway L to reach town hall of **La Mulatière** (4.5km, 166m) in Pl Général Leclerc.

Continue ahead on road beside motorway (D315) and cross river Yzeron into Ave Jean Jaurès. Follow road through **Oullins** (accommodation, refreshments, station) and continue on cycle track beside road over railway bridge into **Pierre-Bénite** (7km, 169m) (accommodation, refreshments, station).

Follow main road through town (now Bvd de l'Europe, D315) on cycle lane R to reach roundabout. Take third exit, using short cycle track to cross to L of road and continue on cycle track L of road over motorway bridge. Go ahead over roundabout into **Irigny** (refreshments, station) and continue through town (Rue d'Yvours, D315), going ahead at three roundabouts. ◀ After third roundabout, cycle lane crosses to R and continues past Vieux Port (refreshments) with railway line L. Road becomes Rue de la Damette, then Rue des Selettes to

Cycling on the main road is prohibited through Irigny: use the cycle track on the left.

166

pass through Les Selettes. Go straight ahead at roundabout (Rte de Vernaison) and continue (road becoming Rte de Lyon) into **Vernaison** (14km, 176m) (accommodation, refreshments, station).

Go ahead over roundabout, then at second roundabout with St Denis parish church R, turn L (Rue du Pont, D36, second exit, sp Solaize). Go ahead over railway crossing and Pont de Vernaison suspension bridge over Rhone onto wooded Île de Sénozan. Fork L, using cycle track R of road, and continue on Pont de Solaize bridge over Rhone Dérivation canal to reach roundabout.

Provisional waymarked route

Turn sharply R at roundabout (first exit) then immediately R again into car park. At end of car park, pass through barriers and bear L downhill on rough gravel cycle track parallel with canal and follow this for 3.5km. Emerge on road, turning R through barrier of boulders, then bear L over motorway bridge. Go ahead over main road onto Rue de la Gare and pass under railway bridge, then zig-zag R and L steeply uphill to reach roundabout in **Ternay** (19.5km, 181m).

Turn R (first exit), then fork R onto side road (Chemin du Port). Where this ends, continue ahead through barrier on gravel cycle track. Emerge on road (Montée de la Monnaie) and bear R to reach small roundabout. Go ahead (first exit) under motorway, then turn R (Rte de Gravignan) over railway bridge. Turn L at T-junction (Rue du 27 Juillet 1944) where alternative route re-joins.

Alternative route avoiding rough trail

Turn L at roundabout (second exit) on road between industrial estate R and motorway L. Follow this to reach large turning circle where off-road and alternative routes briefly coincide. Continue ahead and bear L over motorway bridge to reach main road (Rte de Givors, D312). Turn R, between railway L and motorway R. At oblong-shaped roundabout turn L (Rue du 27 Juillet 1944) uphill, re-joining waymarked route at next road junction.

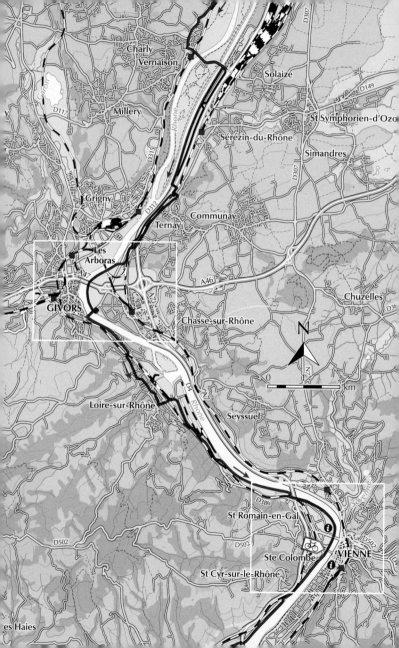

Combined route continues

Follow Rue du 27 Juillet 1944 winding downhill to T-junction. Go ahead onto cycle track and follow this, turning L beside Rhone. Pass under two bridges, then immediately after third bridge turn L away from river and L again on Pont du Chasse 19th-century suspension bridge over river to reach **Givors** (24.5km, 159m) (accommodation, refreshments, cycle shop, station).

First established by the Romans, **Givors** (pop 20,000) sits at the mouth of the Gier valley through which first a canal (1781) then a railway (1830) and latterly a motorway were built, linking Lyon with the industrial city of St Étienne and also connecting the Rhone and Loire valleys. Coal from the Gier valley fuelled the growth of heavy industry around Givors, particularly metallurgical and glass-making companies. Since the 1960s most of this industry has closed and the town is nowadays a dormitory town for Lyon.

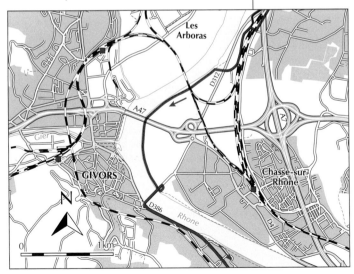

This street, named after two Americans executed (1953) for passing nuclear secrets to Russia, reflects a leftist tendency in Givors going back to the 1848 revolution.

On opposite bank, turn L on Quai Rosenberg. ◀ Follow road (now Ave Anatole France) bearing away from river passing Lidl supermarket L and turn R (Rue Gabriel Péri, sp église du XIIème) at traffic lights. Cross railway bridge and fork L (Rue Renée Peillon). Continue to mini-roundabout and turn half-L (Rue 8 Mai 1945, third exit). Tun R at T-junction (still Rue 8 Mai 1945), then go ahead over crossroads into Rue du Centre. Turn R at roundabout (Rue Edmond Cinquin, first exit) in **Loire-sur-Rhône** (28km, 167m) (refreshments).

Turn L at T-junction (Rue Étienne Flachy, sp Vienne) passing modern town hall L. Go ahead over two crossroads and pass under railway bridge. Bear R past sports club R then keep R on cycle track and follow it past roundabout alongside Rue de Provence. Cycle track crosses to L then bears L away from road and R along riverbank.

To reach Vienne, turn right from the quay (Pl Aristide Briand) then left (Rue Cochard) and left again (Rue Paul Doumer) over Pont de Ste Colombe pedestrian/ cycle bridge.

Turn R on bridge over side stream then L beside road (Quai de Rhône). Pass under motorway bridge then continue beside river and pass under road bridge with St Romain-en-Gal Gallo-Roman museum beside bridge R. Pass church R to reach war memorial R on Quai d'Herbouville in **Ste Colombe** (35.5km, 152m) (accommodation, refreshments, tourist office, station) opposite city of **Vienne** (accommodation, refreshments, tourist office, cycle shop, station). ◀

The capital of the Allobroges, a Celtic tribe, **Vienne** (pop 30,000) was captured by Julius Caesar (47BC) and transformed into a provincial Roman capital. Many Roman artefacts remain, particularly the temple of Augustus and Livia, erected by Claudius, which survived after it became an early Christian church; a truncated pyramid from the Roman hippodrome; and a Gallo-Roman open-air theatre that seated 10,000 spectators. Vienne has been a religious centre since its first bishop was appointed (AD314). After being upgraded to an archbishopric (about AD450), with the title 'primate of all the Gauls', the archbishop became the principal source of authority in the city

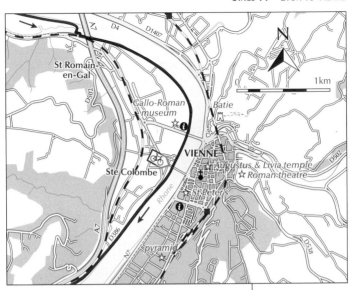

St Maurice cathedral in Vienne

The Plan de l'Aiguille, a Roman pyramid in Vienne, was part of a Roman hippodrome

and remained so for 1000 years. During this time, Vienne was nominally controlled by Burgundians, Franks, the Kingdom of Provence and Arles before becoming part of France in 1449. Religious buildings include the fifth-century St Peter's church, one of the oldest Christian buildings in France, St Maurice cathedral, which rises above a square facing the Rhone, and the St André-le-Bas Benedictine abbey. A ruined medieval castle, Château de la Bâtie, and Chapelle Notre Dame de Pipet sit on separate hills overlooking the city.

STAGE 12

Vienne to Sablons

Start	Vienne, Ste Colombe quayside (152m)
Finish	Sablons bridge (139m)
Distance	33km
Waymarking	ViaRhôna EV17

Continuing south, this completely level stage closely follows the west bank of the Rhone mostly along flood dykes and riverside tracks, with the terraced vineyards of Côte-Rôtie and Condrieu climbing up the valley side.

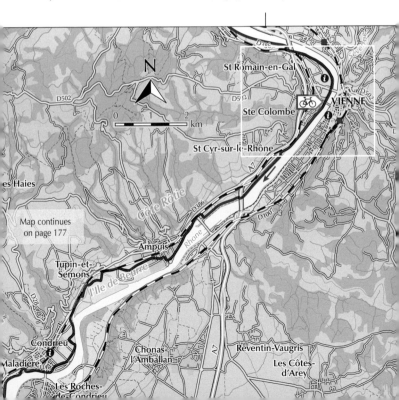

Map continues on page 177

Château Ampuis has been restored by the owners of the Guigal winery

From Quai d'Herbouville in **Ste Colombe**, follow riverside road SW under Pont de Ste Colombe bridge. Continue out of village on cycle track between D386 R and Rhone L to reach **St Cyr-sur-le-Rhône** (accommodation, refreshments). Dog-leg L and R to continue along riverbank, then pass under motorway bridge turning R away from river then L on road beside drainage ditch. Where this reaches a road junction, turn R away from river between industrial units and then L at T-junction beside railway. Pass under road bridge and turn L through barriers to continue on riverside track. Emerge onto road (Ch des Coutures), continuing beside river, then follow Rue du Grand Pré to reach **Ampuis** (6.5km, 150m) (accommodation, refreshments, cycle shop), with Château Ampuis L. ◄

The hillside rising to the right is Côte-Rôtie, an area of vineyards producing high-quality red wine.

Turn R opposite château entrance (Ave du Château) and first L (Rue du Vagnot). Go ahead at crossroads and fork R (Rue de la Plaine) to leave village past greenhouses. Continue beside railway R to reach T-junction beside level crossing in **Tupin-et-Semons** (refreshments). Turn L away from railway over stone bridge and R at T-junction. Turn R on small bridge over backwater and follow track winding through woodland of **l'Ile de Beurre** nature reserve passing a series of viewing hides L. Bear R over stream and turn L emerging on riverbank. After 400m, fork R away from river, and turn L at T-junction to reach hamlet of l'Ile des Pêcheurs. Turn R beside river and continue into Ch de la Plaine. Dog-leg L and R to continue beside drainage canal then emerge onto road and pass under road bridge in **Condrieu** (12.5km, 145m) (accommodation, refreshments, camping, tourist office, cycle shop). ▶

Continue on riverside cycle track (Ruelle des Terreaux). Follow cycle track turning R away from river, then dog-leg R and L onto Ch de Moulin. Turn L beside D386 over bridge, passing river jousting basin L, into **La Maladière** (accommodation, refreshments). ▶ Turn L again along small street (Rue Beau Rivage) passing hotel L. Just past hotel car park, fork L through barriers onto riverbank. Continue over small bridge (entering Loire département) and follow cycle track out of village along riverbank with main road R and vineyards on hillside rising behind. Continue winding through riverside woodland, then back beside river to reach two tall riverside pillars at **Chavanay** (18.5km, 142m) (accommodation, refreshments, cycle shop). The two pillars that look like Egyptian obelisks are suspension towers, all that remain

Condrieu has an annual sculpture competition for compositions in wood, with the winning entries displayed along the towpath.

For more about river jousting, see Serrières below.

The suspension bridge at Chavanay was destroyed in the Second World War, but the towers remain

of a suspension bridge destroyed by retreating German forces in 1944. Continue along riverbank, then detour briefly away from river to cross sidestream beside D1086 before returning to riverbank cycle track. Pass under road bridge, then dog-leg immediately R and L to continue alongside drainage ditch. Dog-leg L and R at next little bridge over ditch to continue on riverbank, with **St Alban** nuclear power station on opposite bank. After 2km emerge beside road (D503) then follow track circling around car park and crossing **St Pierre-de-Bœuf** dam (24km, 139m) (refreshments, gîte, camping, cycle shop).

Continue beside road for 6km, with Rhône canalisé L and **l'Ile de la Platière** nature reserve R, making two dog-legs en route, first around drainage canal then later under road bridge. Where asphalt track beside canal ends, bear R on quiet road (Rue des Granges) between fields and orchards. Pass residential area L and turn R (Ch des Graves) at crossroads, following this bearing L to reach T-junction. Turn L (Rue Robinson) into Les Granges. Turn L again at next T-junction (Rte du Péage, D4) and fork R at roundabout to reach small roundabout by bridge in **Sablons** (33km, 139m) (refreshments). ◀

To visit Serrières (accommodation, refreshments, tourist office) turn right across bridge over Rhone.

SERRIÈRES

The small town of Serrières (pop 1150) has existed since Roman times, but prospered mainly during the 17th–19th centuries as a centre for commercial boats carrying goods on the Rhone, many of the inhabitants being employed as sailors. The introduction from the mid-19th century of steamships that could steam upriver without stopping ended this trade. Modern-day residents reflect this history of boatmanship through river jousting. Although this sport is believed to have originated in Roman times and was practised in medieval France, its current incarnation dates from the late 19th-century introduction of societies of *sauveteurs* (lifeboat men) in riverside towns. The main objective of these societies is to rescue people from the river and aid residents during floods. However, they also organise water sports competitions. These include water jousting, where two boatmen with lances attempt to knock each other from their boats. Serrières is one of the leading centres for this sport. The river basin has been terraced with 2000 viewing seats and has hosted the French championships on a number of occasions.

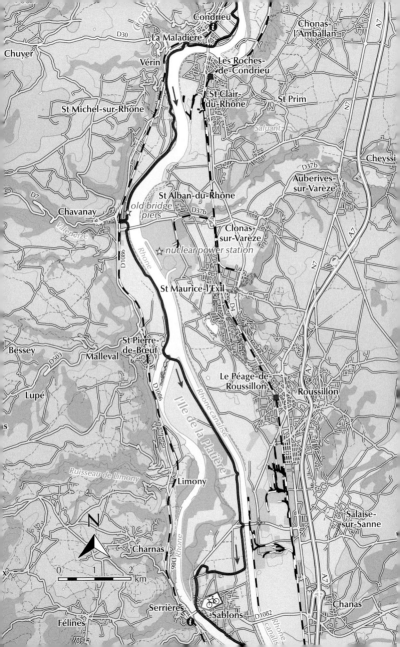

STAGE 13
Sablons to Tournon-sur-Rhône

Start	Sablons bridge (139m)
Finish	Tournon-sur-Rhône bridge (125m)
Distance	36km
Waymarking	ViaRhôna EV17

Still heading south, the route first follows riverside tracks along the east bank, past orchards and small industrial towns, before crossing the Rhone to enter Ardèche département. Here the valley narrows and the stage continues with wooded hillsides coming down close to the river. The last of these slopes on the east is the vineyard covered hill of Crozes-Hermitage. This is a generally level stage apart from one very short climb above the river.

From bridge in **Sablons**, follow Quai de Château SE along riverbank passing small square L. Continue on Quai du Rhône and follow this bearing L away from river. Fork R (Rue Molly Sabata) through open country with Rhone R. Bear R (Ch de Castors), and turn R beside car park onto riverside cycle track. Bear L away from river, then cross road and turn R at second road (Rte de l'Écluse). Follow this bearing L over Sablons dam and lock. Cross bridge over sidestream, then turn R at crossroads (Rue de la Planche) and immediately R through barriers onto cycle track. Pass timber yard L then continue under railway bridge and along riverbank passing below **St Rambert-d'Albon** (5km, 135m) (refreshments, camping, station).

Emerge onto road (Rte du Port-de-Champagne) and continue beside river past **Port de Champagne**. Where this road turns L away from river, continue on cycle track beside river. After 2km, bear L through orchards then turn R onto road (D431) (accommodation). Continue with railway L, past site of former St Gobain glassworks R. Just before reaching main road, turn R (Rue des Clots) and

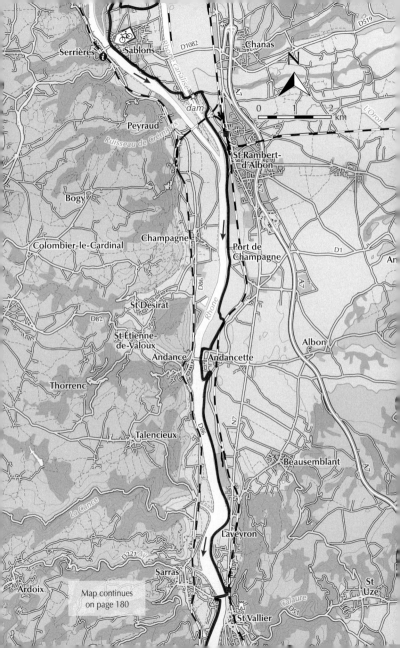

Serrières
Sablons
Chanas
D1082
N7
dam
Peyraud
St-Rambert-
d'Albon
Ruisseau de Crémieux
N7
Bogy
Champagne
Port de
Champagne
D1
Colombier-le-Cardinal
D86
A7
Ar
St Desirat
D82
Rhône
St-Étienne-
de-Valoux
Albon
Andance
Andancette
Thorrenc
Talencieux
N7
D86
Beausemblant
A7
la Cance
Laveyron
D227
St
Uzé
Sarras
Map continues
on page 180
Ardoix
Galaure
D51
St Vallier

Map continues
on page 180

N

0   1   2
km

L'Oron

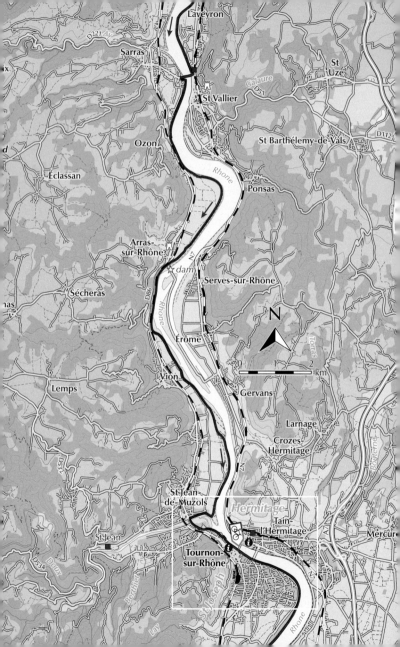

follow this to reach riverbank. Bear L (Quai Christophe) and continue past **Andancette** (11.5km, 131m) (accommodation, refreshments) on Quai Gambetta under Andance suspension bridge.

Follow cycle track bearing L beside wooden benches alongside sidestream to reach T-junction. Turn R over small bridge and R again to regain riverside cycle track. Continue for 6.5km, passing large paper works and tile works (both L) and past **Laveyron** (16.5km, 130m) (refreshments). Pass campsite L and emerge onto road beside landing stage R. Bear R (Rue du Belvédère) to reach **St Vallier** bridge (18.5km, 127m) (accommodation, refreshments, camping, cycle shop, station).

> **St Vallier** (pop 4000) is situated at the confluence of rivers Rhone and Galaure. Originally a Roman settlement, it developed into a medieval walled town. The castle, which has four corner towers and is surrounded by a landscaped garden, was the home of Diane de Poitiers (1499–1566), the mistress of French King Henri II. She wielded much power in court, and when Henri died in a tournament his lance was carrying Diane's ribbon rather than his wife's. In the 18th century, discovery of kaolin (china clay) deposits led to the manufacture of porcelain, a trade that continues with the production of tiles and ceramic insulators.

Turn L beside bridge up steps with ramp for pushing cycles, then R (D886) across bridge over Rhone to reach **Sarras** (accommodation, refreshments). Turn sharply L after bridge and follow Rue du Rhône down to riverbank then turn R on riverside cycle track. After 1.7km, zigzag R and L up to road and continue on cycle track beside road L. Where road bears R under railway bridge, continue ahead on cycle track beside drainage canal parallel with river for 4km. Go ahead across road leading to **Arras** dam (25.5km, 126m) and continue on cycle track between drainage canal L and railway R. After 2km, turn L at T-junction (Ch de Varogne) (accommodation, camping)

Ignore all the side tracks in the woods and stay on the light-coloured asphalt track.

on quiet road through orchards and bear R parallel with river. After 2.5km, fork L on cycle track into woods and continue winding through woods for 3.5km. ◄

Follow track bearing R away from river to reach open area with sports club R. Fork L on cycle track along narrow flood dyke and cycle steeply up short ramp to reach main road (Ave de Lyon, D86). Turn L on cycle track L and cross bridge over river Doux. Pass site of former textile mill L to reach roundabout and turn L. Fork immediately R (Promenade Roche Defrance) on cycle track and follow this past campsite L. Where this ends at large tree-lined square, turn L opposite post office and follow marked cycle track clockwise around square to reach riverbank, then bear R to reach suspension bridge in **Tournon-sur-Rhône** (36km, 125m) (accommodation, refreshments, gîte, camping, tourist office, cycle shop). ◄

Turn left over the bridge to reach Tain-l'Hermitage (accommodation, refreshments, camping, tourist office, cycle shop, station).

The vineyards of l'Hermitage produce some of the highest-quality Rhone wine

The towns of **Tournon-sur-Rhône** (pop 10,600) and **Tain-l'Hermitage** (pop 6100) face each other across a narrow part of the Rhone valley, with steep hills rising on both sides. Tournon, the older and larger

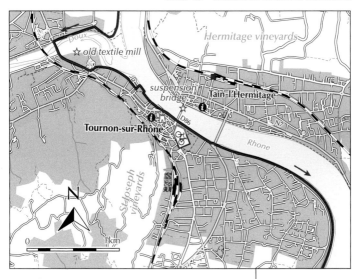

town, developed around a medieval castle with a
walled centre and four monasteries. It is connected
to Tain-l'Hermitage by two bridges, the older of
which is a suspension bridge built in 1825, making
it the oldest in continental Europe. The other fac-
tor linking both towns is wine, St Joseph AC from
the hillside above Tournon and the highly regarded
Hermitage AC from the great south-facing slope
of l'Hermitage hill that dominates the east side of
the valley. Made exclusively from syrah grapes,
Hermitage is one of the highest quality and most
expensive of Rhone wines. On the other side of
the same hill, Crozes-Hermitage produces cheaper,
more accessible wine.

STAGE 14
Tournon-sur-Rhône to Valence

Start	Tournon-sur-Rhône bridge (125m)
Finish	Valence, monumental fountain (128m)
Distance	24km
Waymarking	ViaRhôna EV17

The Rhone valley widens below Tain-l'Hermitage as the east bank opens onto the flood plain of the Isère river. This short, level stage follows flood dykes and riverside roads on the west bank, then crosses the river to follow the towpath of the Rhône canalisé past the confluence of Rhone and Isère. The route eventually leaves the riverbank to end in the centre of Valence, the gateway to the South of France.

The frieze by the roundabout depicts General Rampon, a locally born hero who rose through the ranks to become a general in Napoléon's army and a member of the French senate.

Continue SE from pedestrian bridge in **Tournon-sur-Rhône** on cycle track beside Quai Charles de Gaulle (D86) to reach roundabout beside road bridge. ◀ Continue along riverbank (Quai Gambetta) then where this road

Frieze in Tournon commemorating General Rampon

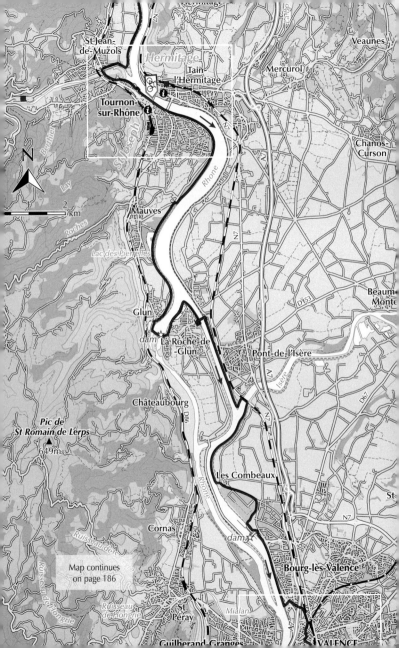

N

2 km

Hermitage

St-Jean-de-Muzols

Veaunes

Tain-l'Hermitage

Mercurol

Tournon-sur-Rhône

Chanos-Curson

Rhône

Mauves

Beaum-Monte

Lac des Pierrelles

Glun

La Roche-de-Glun

dam

Pont-de-l'Isère

Châteaubourg

Pic de St Romain de Lerps
649m

Les Combeaux

St

Cornas

dam

Bourg-lès-Valence

Map continues
on page 186

St Péray

Mialan

VALENCE

Guilherand-Granges

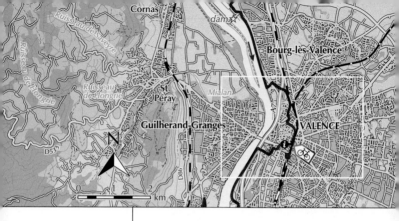

bears away from river continue on riverside cycle track past series of factories R. After 3km turn R across drainage ditch and L on cycle track for another 3.5km, passing **Mauves** (5.5km, 116m) and Pierrelles lake (both R). Emerge onto road (Ch de l'Île) in **Glun** and just after church R, bear L on cycle track beside drainage canal R. Fork L at path junction and zigzag L and R onto flood dyke. Where cycle track ends, continue ahead on road across Glun dam. At roundabout after dam, turn L (Quai des Marettes, third exit, sp Plan d'Eau). Go ahead over small roundabout (Rue de la Traille) then fork L onto track along flood dyke. Follow this bearing R around outside of **La Roche-de-Glun** (9km, 117m) (refreshments, camping).

Pass under bridge then turn immediately R and sharply R again (Ave du Vercours) to cross Rhône canalisé. Immediately over bridge, fork R on cycle track beside road then turn back sharply R to reach canal bank. Turn L beside canal and follow towpath past turn-off L for **Pont-de-l'Isère** (13km, 117m) (accommodation, refreshments) to reach confluence point between rivers Rhone and Isère. Follow towpath back sharply L beside Isère then turn R on new cycle bridge over river. ◄ Turn R on cycle path along opposite bank and where asphalt ends, turn L away from river and R beside road (Rte de Marcerolles, cycle track R) passing **Les Combeaux** L (17.5km, 119m).

Follow cycle track bearing R beside Rte des Combeaux and continue winding through scrubland past

The Isère, the Rhone's second largest tributary, joins the Rhone at Pont-de-l'Isère. Draining the south and west flanks of Mont Blanc, it contributes approximately 20 per cent of the Rhone's flow.

Bourg-lès-Valence locks and dam R. Cross dam approach road then turn L beside canal and continue ahead for 2km. Opposite point where river and canal join, turn L away from river passing between Kyriad hotel L and large car park R, then continue ahead over roundabout and bear R (Rue du Rhône) into **Bourg-lès-Valence** (22km, 111m) (accommodation, refreshments).

Continue ahead at next roundabout (first exit, Rue Gay-Lussac) and follow road over motorway bridge. Go ahead again at next roundabout and follow Rue Gay-Lussac bearing R parallel with railway L. At next roundabout (Pl de la République) take third exit onto dual carriageway (Bvd Général de Gaulle, cycle lane R) and continue uphill into Bvd du Cire. Pass Jardin de la Préfecture behind high walls L and turn L at mini-roundabout past modern *préfecture* (council offices) of Drôme département L. Continue onto dual carriageway (Bvd Vauban) and bear R following bus and cycle lane past statue R of Compte de Montalivet (1766–1823). Pass through bus station to reach monumental fountain on

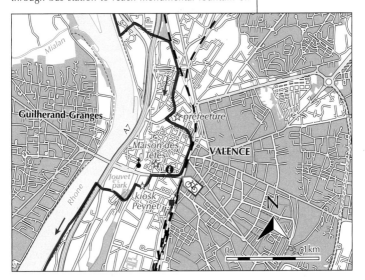

corner of Bvd Bancel in centre of **Valence** (24km, 128m) (accommodation, refreshments, gîte, camping, tourist office, cycle shop, station).

VALENCE

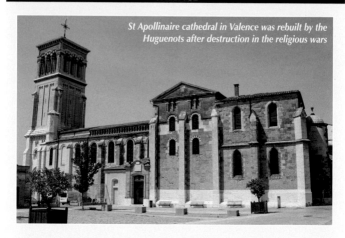

St Apollinaire cathedral in Valence was rebuilt by the Huguenots after destruction in the religious wars

Valence (pop 65,000) regards itself as the gateway to southern France, a claim based on its location near the northernmost limit of olive cultivation. This is reflected in a local saying: *à Valence le Midi commence* ('at Valence the south begins'). The main sights include 11th-century St Apollinaire cathedral, which was badly damaged in the French religious wars and restored in the 17th century. Inside is a monument and the heart of Pope Pius VI (1717–1799) who died here in exile after being deposed when Napoléon captured Rome. The nearby Maison des Têtes is a former 16th-century mansion that derives its name from the many carved heads decorating the façade. In the Champ de Mars is the kiosque Peynet, a highly stylised bandstand, while the nearby Jouvet park has views across the Rhone valley to the hilltop ruins of Château de Crussol. An Armenian church and Armenian museum reflect the 10 per cent of the population of Armenian origin. Local delicacies include the Suisse, an orange-flavoured pastry said to be named after the Pope's Swiss guard. On a higher gastronomic level, restaurant Maison Pic, managed by Anne-Sophie Pic, was the first Michelin three-star restaurant with a female head-chef.

STAGE 15
Valence to Le Pouzin

Start	Valence, monumental fountain (128m)
Finish	Le Pouzin, roundabout (92m)
Distance	33.5km
Waymarking	ViaRhôna EV17

Another level stage. Soon after leaving Valence, the route crosses to the west bank to continue through Ardèche on riverside tracks and quiet roads, with wooded hillsides rising west of the Rhone. After crossing back over the river in La Voulte-sur-Rhône, the route runs through Printegarde nature reserve then follows flood dykes to end in Le Pouzin.

From monumental fountain in **Valence**, cycle W along Bvd Bancel. At beginning of Champ de Mars L, turn L (Pl Championnet) and at gap in trees turn R across Champ de Mars passing beside kiosque Peynet R. At far side of square, descend ramp on L then cross road and bear L downhill (Ave de la Comète) with Jouvet park behind railings R. Follow this road bearing R around side of park and continue across main road onto cycle track opposite. Dog-leg R and L under motorway, then turn L on cycle track beside Rhone. Continue to reach **Port de l'Epervière** (accommodation, refreshments, camping).

Bear L past boatyard R and turn R on cycle track passing marina R. ▶ Continue along riverbank and just before road overbridge turn L away from river. Cross road and after 100m turn R on cycle track. Bear R beside main road and continue across Lônes bridge over Rhone. Follow road for 800m beyond bridge, then turn sharply R on cycle track doubling back beside road. Bear L on winding road parallel with main road (Ch des Basses Fredières, becoming Ch du Ruisseau). Continue almost back to river and opposite house L, fork R under bridge

The wrecked boat abandoned in the river just past the marina is the 'Ardèche', a steam tug that once hauled barges on the Rhone.

*Wreck of 'Ardèche'
steam tug near
Valence marina*

(Ch de Guérimbet, becoming Ch des Acacias). Cross
bridge over drainage canal and turn L between canal L
and railway R. Pass pumping station L then emerge onto
road (Rue du Stade) and continue past **Soyons** (10km,
108m) (accommodation, refreshments).

Continue on Ch du Rhône and 500m after turn-off
for Soyons, fork R between smallholdings. After 500m,
fork R again and follow track through trees bearing L then
curving R onto Ch de l'Ove. After 150m turn sharply L
(Ch du Bac). Continue for 1.4km through orchards and
turn R (Ch de Clairfond) between fields. Turn L beside
railway R then go ahead over crossroads (Ch de Cerisiers)
to reach T-junction in **Charmes-sur-Rhône** (14km, 109m)
(accommodation, refreshments, camping). ◀

*To visit Charmes
turn right under the
railway bridge.*

Turn L (Ch du Bac) and immediately R, past sports
field L and disused station R, to reach T-junction. Turn L
(Rte du Plan d'Eau) beside river Embroye R, passing campsite L. Go ahead at mini-roundabout and turn R (D11)
on bridge over Embroye on cycle track L. Turn second

L on quiet road with drainage ditch L and fields R. After 1.5km, dog-leg R and L then continue with railway R and cross bridge over river Turzon. Continue through industrial area on quayside then go ahead through barriers along cycle track beside Rhone R to reach **Beauchastel** locks and dam (19.5km, 96m).

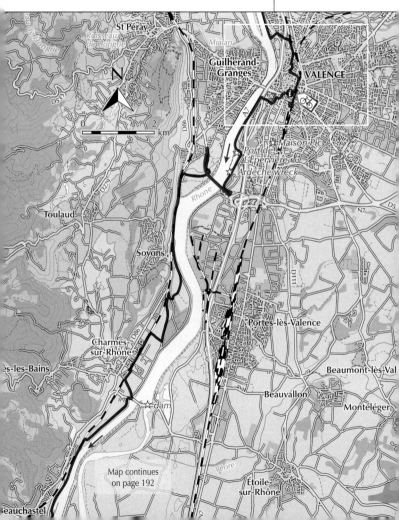

Map continues on page 192

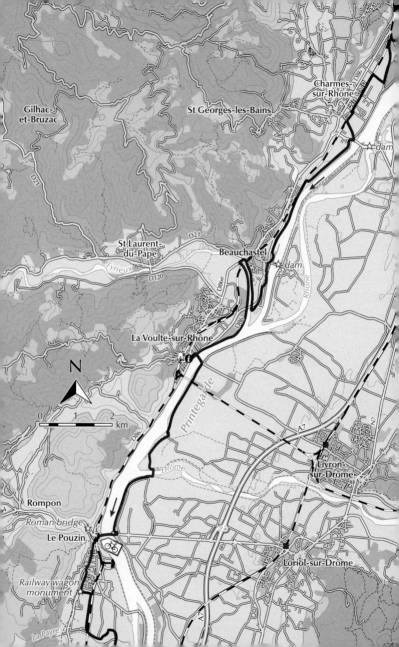

Gilhac-
et-Bruzac

St Georges-les-Bains

Charmes-
sur-Rhône

☆ dam

St Laurent-
du-Pape

Beauchastel

D21

Eyrieux

D120

☆ dam

Rhône

La Voulte-sur-Rhône

D86e

D86

Printegade

N

0   1   2 km

D86

Drôme

Livron-
sur-Drôme

A7

N7

Rompon

Roman bridge

Le Pouzin

Loriol-sur-Drôme

Railway wagon
monument

La Payre

A7

Fork R beside lock, then cross dam approach road and bear L over small bridge, continuing parallel with main road (D86) R. Pass overnight parking area for camper vans and after 150m dog-leg L and R to join riverside cycle track. Follow this winding through woods, eventually re-joining road and turning L. Pass housing blocks L and fork R into woods. Continue to reach river Eyrieux and turn sharply R and continue beside river for 1.3km. Join cycle track behind barriers R, which soon switches to L, and follow this up short bank to pass under railway bridge. Turn L (D86E) on bridge over Eyrieux using cycle track L. At end of bridge turn L on cycle track down to riverbank and pass under railway bridge. Continue under road bridge and follow Rhone for 3km to reach suspension bridge in **La Voulte-sur-Rhône** (26km, 93m) (accommodation, refreshments, tourist office).

St Vincent church and ancient château in La Voulte-sur-Rhône

The narrow streets of the old part of **La Voulte-sur-Rhône** (pop 5000) are clustered at the foot of a rocky limestone outcrop surmounted by a church and ruined castle. Constructed in stages from the 14th–17th centuries, the castle evolved from a military structure into a luxury residence, eventually becoming home to a local industrialist who owned nearby iron ore mines. In August 1944 the castle and the town's two bridges were destroyed by retreating German forces. The bridges have been rebuilt, but the castle remains a ruin. The iron ore mines south west of La Voulte and their associated smelters and furnaces were the main employers. Since their closure a number of high-tech companies have moved into town.

Continue under bridge on cycle track beside road then turn R across main road at crossing before roundabout and immediately R into Pl Étienne Jargeat. Cycle along R side of square and turn R (Rue Thiers, D86F) to cross bridge over Rhône. Immediately after bridge, turn R along quiet riverside road (Ch de Pren te Garde). Pass under railway bridge and continue to reach small dam over Petit Rhône backwater. ◀ Turn L across dam then follow winding cycle track over drainage canal and turn R to continue following Rhône. Bear L away from river through woods, then bear L and turn R to cross bridge over river Drôme. At end of bridge, turn R then zigzag L and R off flood dyke and continue beside river. Bear L past back of Ibis hotel then bear R over hotel entrance road and turn R alongside main road (Rte de Loriol, D104). Cross road at cycle crossing and continue beside road (cycle track L) across bridge over Rhône. Continue under railway bridge to reach roundabout at beginning of **Le Pouzin** (33.5km, 92m) (accommodation, refreshments).

The area between the Rhône and Petit Rhône is Printegarde nature reserve, with many varieties of birds, animals and insects including black kites, storks, bee-eaters, European beaver and 40 varieties of dragonfly.

Le Pouzin (pop 2900) sits astride the entrance to the Ouvèze gorge. The Romans established a small settlement beside the route through the gorge and the bridge they built over the river Ouvèze is still

standing. Later a small medieval castle and walled town were built at the same location. During the religious wars the town was a Protestant stronghold. Captured by Catholic forces, the castle and walls were destroyed. In the Industrial Revolution the town expanded to the south around a foundry that processed iron ore brought down by narrow gauge railway from the Privas basin, although both foundry and railway are long closed.

Flower-bedecked wagons are all that remain of a railway that brought ore to the iron works in Le Pouzin

STAGE 16
Le Pouzin to Montélimar

Start	Le Pouzin, roundabout (92m)
Finish	Montélimar, Pracomtal bridge (73m)
Distance	30km
Waymarking	ViaRhône EV17

This level stage through Ardèche keeps to the west bank of the Rhone with a limestone hillside, much quarried for cement, rising on the right. The route follows roads and field tracks away from the river at first, then joins the riverbank before Cruas and mostly follows the flood dyke to Rochemaure bridge. The river is crossed on a reopened 19th-century 'Himalayan' style footbridge and the route then follows the Rhône canal to Pracomtal bridge opposite the nougat-producing city of Montélimar.

From roundabout at beginning of **Le Pouzin** follow main road S (D86) on cycle lane. After 60m turn R across road then follow cycle track between school buildings and turn L towards river Ouvèze. Zigzag R and L up ramp to cross river bridge. Descend zigzagging L and R then cross road into Rue Victor Hugo. Follow one-way system dog-legging around small square and continue on Rue Victor Hugo. Continue ahead on cycle track beside Ave Jean Claude Dupau (D86) to reach roundabout. Take third exit, going ahead L (D86), with cycle track now L. Follow cycle track bearing L away from road, then cross route of disused narrow gauge railway, with monument of railway wagons R, to emerge on Rue du 8 Mai 1945. After 50m, turn L (Rue George Brassens). At end turn R (Rue Marcel Pagnol) and cycle out of town between railway L and fields R.

At T-junction turn L (Ch de la Payre) under railway bridge on quiet country road, at first following river Payre R then later winding through fields. Turn R (Ch de Plaine)

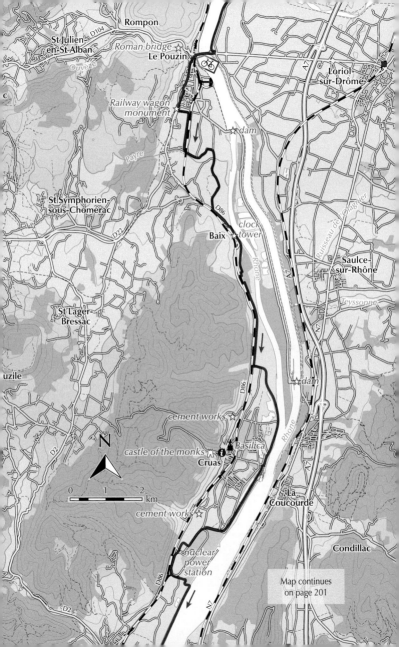

Rompon

St Julien-
en-St-Alban

D104

Roman bridge ☆
Le Pouzin

🚲

Loriol-
sur-Drôme

A7

c

Ouvèze

*Railway wagon
monument*

☆ *dam*

Payre

St Symphorien-
sous-Chomérac

D21

D86

*clock
tower* ☆

Baix

Rhône

Saulce-
sur-Rhône

Ruisseau de la longue

St Lager-
Bressac

N7

Veyssoppe

↓

uzile

D2

D86

☆ *dam*

cement works ☆

Rhône

castle of the monks ☆ 🅰 *Basilica*
ⓘ
Cruas

La
Coucourde

N

0   1   2
|___|___|___| km

cement works ☆

*nuclear
power
station*

D86

↓

N7

Condillac

D2

Map continues
on page 201

at T-junction and fork L to cross Payre using modern cyclists' suspension bridge. Continue winding through fields and orchards to reach main road (D86). Turn L, using cycle track L, to reach **Baix** (7km, 97m) (accommodation, refreshments).

At beginning of village, fork L along narrow village street (Rue Victor Hugo). Turn L after building 42 then bear R behind primary school and continue into Quai du Rhône N. Just before end, bear L beside Rhone and continue into Quai du Rhône S. Pass under archway and emerge into small square (Pl de l'Église) with village church R. Bear L (Rue de Rhône) past red flood marker on wall R and continue on asphalt cycle track out of village through orchards and allotments. Turn R under railway, then L to continue on other side. Dog-leg L and R back under railway and follow cycle track for 2.5km. Cross seasonal ford and turn L at T-junction onto road. Where road turns R, bear L ahead on cycle track, then bear gently R along flood dyke with Rhone L and series of lagoons R. Pass campsite R and reach turn-off R to **Cruas** (14km, 83m) (refreshments, camping, tourist office).

The cycle route passes through the arcaded clock tower in Baix

In the centre of **Cruas** (pop 3000) there is an attractive Catholic basilica, parts of which date back to the eighth century. Inside is a painting marked 'gift of the Emperor', referring to Napoléon Bonaparte. However, the most significant local features are on the limestone hillside that rises west of the valley. The Benedictines built a monastery south of the village, parts of which remain, and to provide protection in times of flood or war they built a fortified chapel and tower on the hillside above the monastery, the ruins being called the 'Castle of the Monks'. Two large cement works (Lafarge and Calcia), also on the hillside, dominate the view. Cement production started in the 1850s using lime from a very pure local outcrop and approximately 400,000 tonnes are produced annually. Beside the Rhone, south of the village, is a large nuclear power station.

Parts of Cruas basilica were built in the eighth century

Turn R over drainage ditch and L on cycle track parallel with ditch. After 2km, bear R beside perimeter fence and drainage canal that surround Cruas nuclear power station. Continue beside perimeter road R with windfarm L, passing roundabout. Cross to R of perimeter road and continue past cooling towers L. Follow cycle track turning R through fields and then L to pass car park and reach main access road to Cruas power station (17.5km, 78m).

Go ahead across access road and follow cycle track beside perimeter road L. Cross railway siding and where road turns R away from power station continue ahead on cycle track. Cross bridge over drainage ditch then turn R and L, following security fence, to reach Rhone. Turn R on cycle track along flood dyke. After 2.25km turn R off dyke across drainage ditch and turn L on cycle track beside ditch. Ignore road forking R, then zigzag R and L over drainage ditch and bear R along flood dyke. Fork R away from Rhone 100m before Rochemaure dam and bear L to reach dam access road (23.5km, 72m).

Turn R away from dam (Ch de Esther) to cross river Lavézon and continue through woods. Turn L on quiet road between woods L and fields R (Ch du Mouton). After 250m, fork L on cycle track through fields and bear R beside riparian woodland. Cycle along riverbank for 800m then follow cycle track bearing R through fields. Continue on Ch de la Jalette, passing sewerage works R with **Rochemaure** castle visible on hilltop ahead. Turn L at T-junction (Ch du Stade), parallel with railway R, to reach second T-junction (25.5km, 72m). ◄

To visit Rochemaure (accommodation, refreshments), turn right at the second T-junction, passing under railway bridge.

Rochemaure (pop 2300), which means black rock, sits on the side of a volcanic intrusion of harder basalt rock standing above the surrounding limestone. The rock is topped by a medieval castle, the walls of which run down the hillside to the town below. The basalt rock has been eroded into organ pipe formations that appear to mimic the fortifications of the castle. On the hillside, the Chapel of Our Lady of the Angels is now a museum. Houses in the village are made with both black basalt and

cement works ☆

castle of the monks

Basilica

Cruas

la
Coucourde

Condillac

cement works ☆

nuclear
power
station

D86

N7

Meysse

Rhone

Savasse

St Marcel

☆ dam

Rochemaure

D2

A7

D6

suspension bridge

Ancone

D86

MONTÉLIMAR

N102

Le Teil

Pracomtal

D540

D86

Lac du
Pont Rouge

D4

MONTÉLIMAR

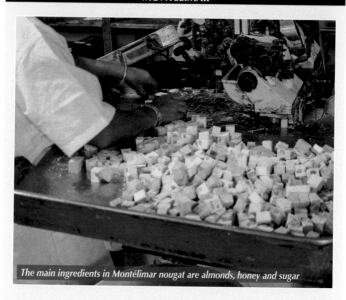

The main ingredients in Montélimar nougat are almonds, honey and sugar

Montélimar (pop 40,000) gets its name from the Adhémar de Monteil family, local rulers who built the 11th-century Adhémar castle which still dominates the cityscape. During the religious wars, Montélimar – at the time a Protestant city – was besieged several times and a citadel was built overlooking the town. In the late 19th century the city walls were pulled down and replaced with a wide boulevard. Modern-day Montélimar is famous for the production of nougat. First produced in the 17th century, soon after almonds had been introduced to the region, Montélimar nougat is a mixture of almonds (30 per cent), lavender honey (25 per cent), sugar, pistachios (two per cent), egg white and vanilla. Production is carried out in large factories and by about 20 small artisanal confectioners, whose factories can be visited. Nougat is one of 13 desserts (symbolising Jesus Christ and his 12 apostles) traditionally served by French families on Christmas Eve.

white limestone. The pedestrian suspension bridge was built in 1859 by Marc Seguin, an early pioneer of suspension bridge design. The three bridge towers were designed to replicate Rochemaure castle, while the deck originally had open wooden slats. Closed in 1978 after a new bridge opened 500m downstream, it was renovated and reopened in 2013 specifically to serve the ViaRhôna.

Turn L away from railway (Allée du Vieux Pont) and continue straight ahead over Pont de Rochemaure 'Himalayan' style pedestrian/cycle suspension bridge across Rhone. It is narrow with open mesh sidewalls, and you may feel more comfortable walking your cycle across. Take extra care in high winds and avoid the bridge during thunderstorms. Follow cycle track bearing L and turning R along flood dyke. Pass under road bridge and follow canal for 2.25km to pass under **Pracomtal** bridge (30km, 73m). ▸

To visit the centre of Montélimar (accommodation, refreshments, tourist office, cycle shop, station) turn right after the bridge then right, and then right again over the bridge, continuing on the main road (N102) for 3km.

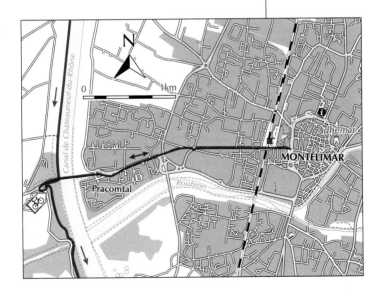

STAGE 17
Montélimar to Pont-St Esprit

Start	Montélimar, Pracomtal bridge (73m)
Finish	Pont-St Esprit, Le Bout-du-Pont roundabout (43m)
Distance	41km
Waymarking	ViaRhôna EV17

This completely level stage follows the west bank of the Rhone past Viviers and through long stretches of riparian woodland to Bourg-St Andéol. It then crosses onto a large island formed between the Donzère–Mondragon canal and the Rhone, following quiet roads down this island through farmland, to end at Le Bout-du-Pont opposite the ancient town of Pont-St Esprit.

From under **Pracomtal** bridge follow cycle track, turning R parallel with bridge approach, then L and R to run beside drainage ditch with Montélimar Dérivation canal behind flood dyke L. After 2km, bear sharply R then cross road and continue (Ch de l'Écluse) on winding cycle track for another 4km, mostly beside drainage ditch. Dog-leg R and L across drainage ditch and continue to reach road. Turn L (D237, cycle track R) and follow road over Henri Poincaré dam (7.5km, 68m).

To reach Châteauneuf-du-Rhône (accommodation, refreshments, camping) continue ahead on road D237).

Bear R to follow cycle track R of parking area, then cross road and follow cycle lane bearing R behind trees. Emerge alongside road, cross drainage canal, then turn R away from road on cycle track beside drainage canal R. ◄ At approach to **Châteauneuf-du-Rhône** bridge, fork L up to bridge and turn R across bridge over Rhone (10.5km, 65m). ◄

To visit Viviers (accommodation, refreshments, camping, tourist office) continue ahead after bridge for 500m.

Viviers (pop 3700) has been an important episcopal city since the fourth century, when it became the seat of an early Christian bishopric. St Vincent's cathedral dates from the 11th–12th centuries, although the vaulted ceiling was re-constructed

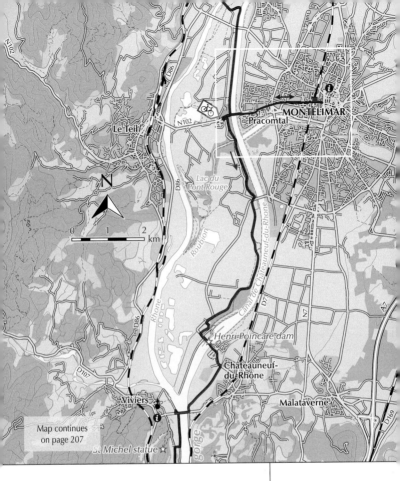

Map continues
on page 207

in the 18th century. In 1856 the bishop acquired six Gobelin tapestries; five are on display but the sixth, which featured the Last Supper, was stolen and is believed to be in a private collection. Other important buildings include the former bishops' palace and the House of the Knights. Outside the town, a multi-arched Roman bridge crosses the river Escoutay.

A statue of Archangel Michael (St Michel) sits atop a limestone ridge overlooking the Rhone near Viviers

Immediately after bridge, turn R then R again on cycle track under bridge and along riverside. After 1km follow this R away from river and turn L at T-junction of tracks. Continue with first limestone cliffs R, topped by statue of Archangel Michael (St Michel in French), then flood dyke R of road. Emerge on riverbank. Follow river, with sheer white limestone cliffs of Donzère gorge rising on opposite side of Rhone, to reach approach road for Pont du Robinet bridge.

Dog-leg across road past old stone tower beside bridge and continue beside flood dyke for 400m. Bear R away from river then L beside drainage canal and follow cycle track winding through riparian woodland. Turn R beside approach road to **Donzère** dam (16km, 65m).

Dog-leg under dam approach road and continue along flood dyke with river L on cycle track winding through woodland. After 5km, turn R away from riverbank, then turn L across new bridge over Lône de la Grande Écrasée stream. Follow cycle track winding through fields and woods to emerge on quiet road. Bear

St home

D107

Châteauneuf-
du-Rhône

Viviers ★

Malataverne

St Michel statue ★

D86

Donzère gorge

D844

N

0　　1　　2
━━━━━━━ km

Donzère

A7

dam

St Montan

dam

D86

Conche

Rhone

Lône Cadérousse

D144

A7

Berre

D93n

La Garde-
Adhémar

D86

D458

Pierrelatte

D358

Bourg
St Andéol

Tourne valley

Plan d'eau de Pigne dorée

A7

Map continues
on page 208

L Seignan

R following road away from river. Cross Grande Écrasée again and turn sharply L beside trees L past ruined farm building L. ▶ Follow track beside stream, then bear R through allotments. Emerge onto road and bear L. Pass under road bridge and fork L on cycle track parallel with main road (D86) passing Palais des Évêques (bishops' palace) R to reach **Bourg-St Andéol** R (26.5km, 54m) (accommodation, refreshments, camping, tourist office).

Ruined building has been kept as a memorial to the victims of a great flood in 1796.

Bourg-St Andéol (pop 7200) is a town of religious buildings, patricians' house and decorative fountains. The oldest artefact is a Roman bas relief of the God Mithra, a popular cult figure during the second and third centuries AD. The former church of St Polycarpe housed the tomb and relics of St Andéol, a Christian missionary sent to convert Gaul, who was martyred by the Romans in AD208. The carved sarcophagus of the tomb is now in St Andéol parish church but the relics were destroyed during

The ancient carved Sarcophagus in Bourg-St Andéol

the French Revolution. Other religious buildings include the bishops' palace and three former monasteries. In the Tourne valley, below limestone cliffs, local springs were tapped and used to supply drinking water fountains in the town. The most notable fountain is a monument to Lady Vierne Balazuc who gave a communal forest to the town. The proceeds from exploiting the timber were used to provide street lighting, making it the first provincial French town so equipped.

Pass under Bourg-St Andéol bridge then turn immediately R, ascending to bridge, and continue across Rhone (D86K, becoming D59 in Drôme). On opposite bank, follow cycle track R of road and turn R at crossroads (Ch de la Calamelle). Pass aggregates depot R and fork R (Ch de Joncs), passing aggregate lagoons R, and continue to reach overhead power line. Fork R (still Ch de Joncs) and continue with flood dyke L and drainage ditch R. Climb over flood dyke and continue winding through fields. Pass industrial estate L and turn sharply R (Ch de Barrinques) 50m before reaching dual carriageway main road on outskirts of **Lapalud** (35km, 45m). ◄

To reach Lapalud town centre (accommodation, refreshments, camping) continue ahead over the main road.

Continue on winding road beside drainage ditch R for 3km to reach T-junction. Turn R over drainage ditch and continue with trees surrounding chateau L and fields R. Bear R over river Lauzon, then bear R at T-junction (D63) to reach roundabout in **Le Bout-du-Pont** (41km, 43m) (refreshments). ◄

To visit Pont-St Esprit (accommodation, refreshments, gîte, camping, tourist office), turn R (first exit, D994) and continue across bridge over Rhone.

PONT-ST ESPRIT

The eponymous 20-arch stone bridge at Pont-St Esprit

Pont-St Esprit (pop 10,400) is situated just below the confluence of the Ardèche and Rhone rivers. Named after the 20-arch Rhone bridge, built in 1265, its position at the junction of Auvergne-Rhône-Alpes, Occitanie and Provence-Alpes-Côte d'Azur regions has led to the soubriquet 'gateway to Provence'. The skyline is dominated by two churches, St Pierre (ninth century) and St Saturnin (15th century). The town was the home of Michel Bouvier, great-grandfather of Jacqueline Bouvier who first married US president John Kennedy then after his assassination married Greek shipping magnate Aristotle Onassis.

STAGE 18
Pont-St Esprit to Avignon

Start	Pont-St Esprit, Le Bout-du-Pont roundabout (43m)
Finish	Avignon, Centre station (19m)
Distance	56.5km
Waymarking	ViaRhôna EV17

Keeping east of the Rhone, closely following the river on quiet roads and riverside cycle tracks, this completely flat stage takes you into Provence. The route passes below the wine-producing village of Châteauneuf-du-Pape then crosses Oiselay island before ending in the historic papal capital of Avignon.

Opened in 1952 as part of the Donzère dam hydroelectric scheme, the Donzère–Mondragon canal is the Rhone's main navigable channel.

To visit Mondragon (accommodation, refreshments) follow main road forking L over motorway.

Follow road (D994) W in **Le Bout-du-Pont** and fork R towards Rhone. Turn sharply L under bridge with flood meadows R then fork R before farm to pass under second road bridge. After 250m, turn L beside orchard then cross flood dyke and turn R at crossing of tracks. Continue to reach flood dyke and bear L beside dyke. After next bend, fork L away from dyke on quiet road winding through fields. Pass under TGV high-speed railway and go ahead over crossroads. Turn L beside canal and R on bridge over Canal de Donzère–Mondragon. ◄ Follow main road (D44) bearing R at roundabout then fork R (Ch des Cadhérines, sp Mornas) to by-pass **Mondragon** (5.5km, 42m). ◄

Turn L at T-junction then bear R beside A7 motorway. Turn L over river Lez, then go ahead R at crossroads to continue beside motorway. Bear R away from motorway then turn L at crossroads to return to motorway. Bear R and follow motorway for 2.5km with Mornas fortress dominating the clifftop L. Bear R away from motorway again then turn L (Ch du Moulas) at T-junction. Fork R (Ch des Pièces) before motorway and continue to small roundabout in **Mornas** (11km, 35m) (accommodation, refreshments).

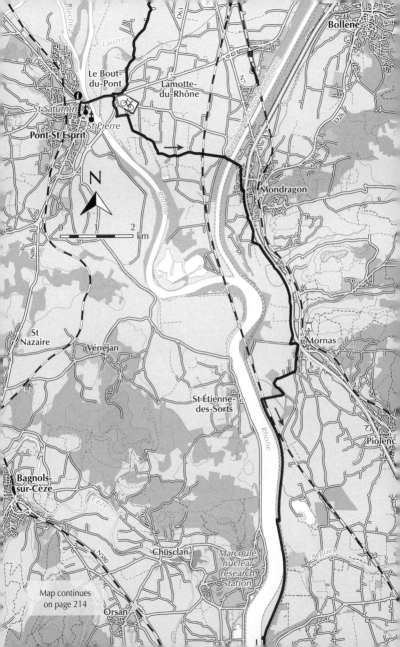

Bollène

Le Bout-du-Pont

Lamotte-du-Rhône

St-Saturnin

St Pierre

Pont-St-Esprit

Canal de Donzère Mondragon

N

0   1   2 km

Rhône

Mondragon

St Nazaire

Vénéjan

Mornas

St-Étienne-des-Sorts

Rhône

Piolenc

Bagnols-sur-Cèze

Cèze

Chusclan

Marcoule nuclear research station

Aygues

Orsan

Map continues on page 214

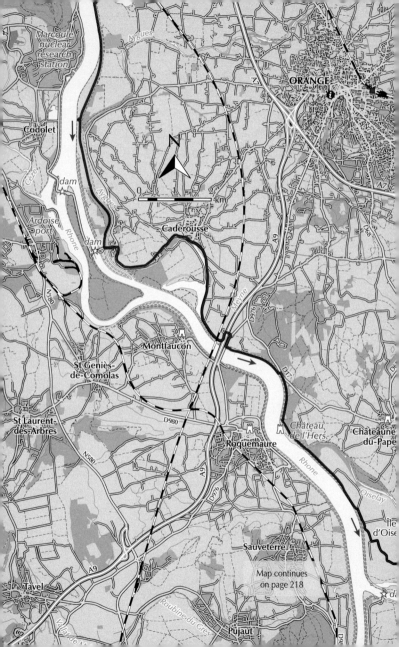

Marcoule nuclear research station

ORANGE

Codolet

dam

Cèze

Ardoise port

Rhône

dam

Aygues

Caderousse

A9

Meyne

D976

D68

A7

N580

Montfaucon

St Geniès-de-Comolas

St Laurent-des-Arbres

D980

Roquemaure

Château de l'Hers

Châteauneuf-du-Pape

D17

N580

A9

D976

Rhône

Oiselay

Île d'Oise

Tavel

Sauveterre

Map continues on page 218

A9

Roubine du Grès

Villard de M

Pujaut

D98

0   km

Standing on top of a 137m cliff and originally the site of a Roman castrum, the 11th-century **Mornas fortress** was built by the Count of Toulouse to control passage via the Rhone gorge and shipping on the river. Later owners included the bishop of Arles and the Pope. During the wars of religion the fortress was hotly contested, and was captured by Calvinists (1562) before re-capture by Catholic forces (1568). After the Revolution, Mornas was abandoned and fell into disrepair. It was declared a historic monument in 1928, and active restoration began in 1977 and is still ongoing.

Bear R (first exit, still Ch des Pièces) then turn R at crossroads (Ch du Paty). Follow this bearing L beside stone flood dyke then turn R over small bridge. Pass under TGV railway bridge and turn L on cycle track beside Rhone flood dyke. Follow this for 3.5km, then dog-leg R and L to climb onto main flood dyke and continue ahead. ▶ Cross over an aggregates conveyor, then dog-leg R and L around an access point to the dyke. Eventually drop down off dyke and dog-leg L and R across gravel track, then bear L beside quiet road through forest. Where trees end, continue to T-junction beside Caderousse dam (23.5km, 31m). Turn L beside D236 over river Aygues and pass La Piboulette L. Go ahead at roundabout and bear R on cycle track into woods. Follow this parallel with road past Cite des Islons to reach edge of **Caderousse** (26.5km, 29m) (accommodation, refreshments). ▶

Continue on cycle track L of road (D237), following this across to R at end of village. Follow Aygues R and continue under bridge carrying TGV high-speed railway line from Paris to Marseille, then bear L and R to pass under motorway bridge and reach roundabout. Go ahead over first exit (D976) and turn R on cycle track L of road. After 300m, follow track bearing L away from road past car park R and join cycle track along Rhone flood dyke. Opposite cruise landing stage for Châteauneuf-du-Pape/ Orange, turn L over drainage ditch and R on opposite bank. At next bridge (accommodation 1km off-route)

The large industrial complex on the opposite bank is Marcoule, the principal research centre for the French nuclear power industry.

A sign at the beginning of Caderousse shows the Provençale dialect spelling: 'Cadarousso'.

Château de l'Hers stands on a rock overlooking the vineyards of Châteauneuf-du-Pape

cross back over drainage channel to R bank, and pass ruined **Château de l'Hers** beside river R (34km, 25m).

The oldest parts of the ruined **Château de l'Hers** date back to the 10th century, although the most visible remains (the round tower and part of the ramparts) were 14th-century additions. Built originally for a bishop of Avignon, it was used to control shipping on the Rhone and collect tolls. Over the centuries it had a number of owners, including the Avignon papacy, all of whom benefited from the toll income. When feudal toll-rights were abolished by the French Revolution, the castle was abandoned and fell into disrepair. The ruins are classified as a national monument and nowadays are owned by a local wine estate producing *appellation contrôlée* Châteauneuf-du-Pape wines.

Where track forks, take R fork nearest to flood dyke. Follow this, soon re-crossing drainage channel onto **Île d'Oiselay** island and continue with vineyards L. At next crossing of tracks, dog-leg L and R onto quiet country road (Ch Île d'Oiselay). Follow this winding through riparian woodland and turn R at T-junction (still Ch Île d'Oiselay) by La Chartreuse. Continue through fields and vineyards then turn L on causeway across Oiselay channel with derelict Arméniers suspension bridge L.

Turn R at T-junction and follow road bearing L to mini-roundabout. Go ahead (Ch Île d'Oiselay, second exit), then pass under motorway to reach second mini-roundabout. Turn R (Pont de l'Ouvèze, first exit) over river Ouvèze and continue ahead (Ave d'Orange). Bear L at another mini-roundabout (Rue du Pontillac, sp Théâtre) to reach Pl de la République in centre of **Sorgues** (43.5km, 23m) (accommodation, refreshments, camping, station).

Continue into Cours de la République and turn R to roundabout. Go ahead L (third exit) and turn immediately L (D6, sp Vedène) through Pl Charles de Gaulle past town hall behind car park R. Go ahead over next roundabout (Ave Achille Maureau, second exit) and continue under railway bridge. Go ahead over next roundabout (Ave Pablo Picasso) then turn R at larger roundabout (Ch de Brantes, sp Poinsard), using cycle lane R. Follow this through industrial area, then where road rises to cross railway bridge, turn L (Ch des Granges). Follow road ahead for 3km, with railway line R, then bear L beside motorway. Go ahead across slip road and follow cycle track forking R. Turn R at mini-roundabout (sp Le Pontet) and go ahead over motorway bridge to reach larger roundabout. Turn L (third exit, sp Le Pontet centre), then at next roundabout, bear R (first exit, sp centre ville) using cycle lane R. Pass prison R and continue ahead over another roundabout (Ave Gustave Goutarel) into Avignon suburb of **Le Pontet** (50km, 22m) (accommodation, refreshments, camping, cycle shop).

Turn L (Ave de l'Église) beside metal cross and pass between Notre-Dame church L and market place R to reach T-junction. Turn R (Ave François Lascour) and first L (Ave du Maréchal de Lattre de Tassigny). At end, turn R (Ave Guillaume de Fargis). Bear R at next T-junction,

continuing to wind through residential area, then pass Château de Fargues L and go ahead over main road into Ave Émile Zola.

> **Château de Fargues** was built for Cardinal William de Fargis, a nephew of Pope Clement V. Nowadays, it is a music conservatory that hosts performances during the Avignon festival.

Immediately before next roundabout, cross road to L and turn L on cycle track beside Rue Gustave Courbet. Go ahead over crossroads (Ave François de Chateaubriand) now using cycle lane R and continue to T-junction. Turn L and immediately fork R into Rue Claude Chabrol. Opposite first pedestrian crossing, turn R on wooden boardwalk over small stream and continue on cycle track beside stream L. Go ahead over crossroads, continuing behind houses R, then dog-leg L over stream and R on tree-lined avenue beside children's playground in Parc Chico Mendes. Turn R beside Rue Georges Braque, then L across road and follow cycle track between houses L and shopping centre R in Avignon suburb of Quartier Est.

Cross main road then turn R on cycle track beside road and follow this bearing L past roundabout beside Ave de la Folie. At second roundabout, continue ahead over first exit to join Chemin des Canaux cycle track and follow this bearing L away from road. Dog-leg L and R over drainage canal then bear R under motorway. Go ahead over crossroads, still following drainage canal, then dog-leg R and L over staggered crossroads, into Ave de St Jean. Pass under two railway bridges and emerge beside Bvd Limbert. ▶ Turn L and immediately R across road at first crossing, then bear L on cycle track through gardens between road L and Avignon city walls R.

Follow this ahead over series of crossroads to reach fourth gateway through walls (Porte de la République) opposite **Avignon** Centre station (56.5km, 19m) (accommodation, refreshments, youth hostel, camping, tourist office, cycle shop, station). ▶

Bvd Limbert is part of a ring of boulevards that circle the outside of Avignon city walls.

To reach historic centre, turn R through gateway and follow Cours Jean Jaurès ahead to reach Pl de l'Horloge.

AVIGNON

Although originally a Phoenician settlement that was captured by the Romans, Avignon (pop 92,000 city, 460,000 metro) is best known for its connection with the papacy during the 14th century. In 1305, when French-born Clement V was elected pope, political tension prevented him from moving to Rome and in 1309 he established Avignon as the capital of his papacy. He was followed by six more 'Avignon Popes' and three 'anti-popes' who resided in Avignon in opposition to the 'true-pope' in Rome. This schism in the Catholic church was ended in 1417 by the Council of Constance. During their reign, the popes built and extended the Palais des Papes and constructed 5km of ramparts with 39 towers that surround the city. As the capital of the church, the city attracted legations, merchants and financiers, bringing great wealth and prosperity. After the pope moved back to Rome, the city and its hinterland remained papal territory governed by a papal legate, not becoming part of France until after the revolution in 1793.

The impressive Palais des Papes was constructed between 1316 and 1379 in Gothic style and stands beside the Romanesque-style Notre-Dame cathedral on Rocher de Doms hill, overlooking Pl du Palais square. The city walls are the best-preserved medieval fortifications in France. In the city centre the *hôtel de ville* (city hall) and clock tower stand in Pl de l'Horloge, surrounded by restaurants. St Bénézet bridge is a ruined bridge, built in 1234 with 22 arches. Although only four arches survive, the rest having been swept away by a flood in 1669, the popular children's song 'Sur le Pont d'Avignon' has made it the city's most famous landmark.

The enormous 14th-century Palais des Papes rises above the city of Avignon

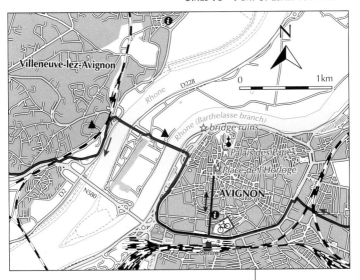

STAGE 19
Avignon to Arles

Start	Avignon, Centre station (19m)
Finish	Arles, Bvd Georges Clemenceau (8m)
Distance	58.5km
Waymarking	ViaRhôna EV17, partly provisional yellow waymarks

After Avignon, this stage crosses to the west bank, at first clinging to the side of the Rhone flood plain with wooded limestone hills rising beside the route. The route passes small towns before reaching the medieval trading town of Beaucaire, then finally crosses a flat agricultural plain to reach the Roman city of Arles. The landscape of this area has achieved fame through the paintings of Vincent van Gogh. Except for a few gentle undulations after leaving Avignon and between Montfrin and Beaucaire, the stage is flat.

From S side of Porte de la République gateway opposite **Avignon** Centre station, cycle W following city walls R past four more gates. After fourth gate follow cycle track ahead through car park and beside main road following route marked on road, then after fifth gate (Porte de l'Oulie) bear L following green marked cycle lane across Bvd du Rhône. Continue ahead (D900) on Pont Édouard d'Daladier and Pont du Royaume bridges over two Rhone channels into **Villeneuve-lez-Avignon** (accommodation, refreshments, youth hostel, camping, tourist office).

The route from Pont du Royaume has provisional waymarks for 5km past Les Angles and as far as the TGV railway bridges. A new route is planned following the Rhone flood dyke.

At end of bridge, follow cycle track bearing slightly R and turn immediately L back to main road using crossing. ◀ Immediately before railway bridge, turn L (Ancienne Rte d'Aramon, becoming Rue du Chêne Vert). Go ahead at roundabout and pass under railway bridge into **Les Angles** (3.5km, 22m) (accommodation). Turn L at crossroads (Bvd du Midi) and continue out of built-up area. At crossroads by major highway, turn R away from highway (still Bvd du Midi). Bear L on tree-lined Ch Louis

Montagne with limestone cliffs rising R and continue under motorway. Road now winds along beside forested hillside R, becoming Ch de la Tuilerie. Pass under two high viaducts that carry branches of the TGV railway line over the Rhone and small stone bridge that carries the old railway.

Go ahead over main road, then turn R on gravel cycle track beside Rhone flood dyke L. Follow this for 6km then emerge on main road just before Aramon bridge. ▶

Cross road using crossing then take second exit at roundabout, going through barriers onto cycle track. Turn R at first crossroads, passing under railway bridge, then turn L (Ch du Mas Rouge) uphill beside railway. At next junction, turn L back under railway and go ahead over roundabout (Lotissement de Sarments, second exit).

Sanofi chemical works, on opposite side of railway, produces pharmaceuticals from plant and vegetable extracts.

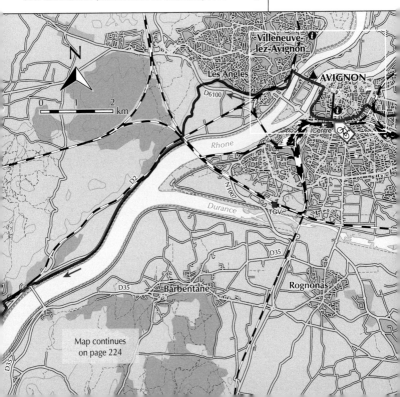

Map continues on page 224

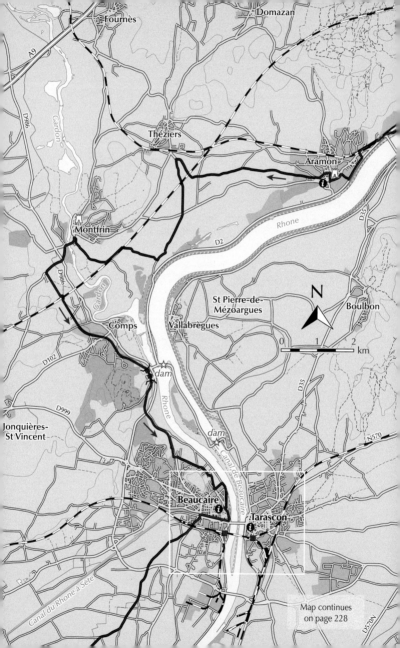

Fournès

Domazan

Thèziers

Aramon

Montfrin

Gardon

Rhone

D2

St Pierre-de-Mézoargues

Boulbon

N

0   1   2 km

Comps

Vallabrègues

dam

Rhone

Jonquières-St Vincent

dam

Canal de Beaucaire

Beaucaire

Tarascon

Canal du Rhône à Sète

Map continues
on page 228

Follow this bearing R and becoming Ch du Rhône. Turn R beside house 217 (still Ch du Rhône) and continue to T-junction. Turn L (Ave Jean Moulin), parallel with Aramon city walls R. Turn R at roundabout (first exit, sp Centre Historique) through gateway into **Aramon** (16km, 15m) (accommodation, refreshments, tourist office).

Continue ahead (Bvd Gambetta) through narrow streets of old town and turn L (Ave de la Libération) at staggered crossroads. At second crossroads, fork R after house 26, then fork L (Ch du Mas Neuf) by wayside cross R. Pass through flood dyke and continue through vineyards. Bear L at junction of tracks then go ahead over crossroads and pass under railway bridge to reach T-junction (21km, 10m). ▶

To visit Théziers (accommodation) turn R at T-junction.

Turn L and continue under another railway bridge and over crossroads. After 3km, turn R through vineyards and pass under railway for third time. Immediately after bridge, turn L beside railway. Follow quiet road bearing R away from railway to reach junction and fork L through trees. Bear L past boules piste R to reach T-junction on edge of **Montfrin** (27km, 12m) (accommodation, refreshments). ▶

To reach town centre, turn R at T-junction and go ahead over roundabout.

Turn L and follow road over river Gardon. Immediately after bridge, bear L (D264, sp Beaucaire) in Faubourg du Pont to reach roundabout. Go ahead uphill (D763, second exit, sp Jonquières) and after 600m turn L onto Voie Verte du Pont-du-Guard cycle track along former railway trackbed. Dog-leg L and R under TGV railway bridge and continue past old station in **Comps** (31km, 19m).

Pass through short (200m) tunnel under Mont Aiguille to reach end of cycle track on outskirts of Beaucaire. Turn L to roundabout and go ahead (Ch de Marguilliers, second exit, sp Champ de Foire). Follow this to crossroads just before car park for Roman arena and turn L beside arena R. Turn R at T-junction and continue beside Rhone L. Where road forks, keep L beside river, passing below Beaucaire castle above R. Pass casino R and turn second R across casino car park and through gateway in city walls. Turn immediately L

The road around the canal basin is a large one-way system, making it necessary to cycle round the north and west sides. | (Rue Danton) with city wall L and continue into Rue Frederic Mistral. After building 1, fork R (Sq Eysette). At end turn R (Quai Général de Gaulle) along N side of canal du Rhône à Sète basin in middle of **Beaucaire** (38.5km, 5m) (accommodation, refreshments, tourist office, station). ◀

BEAUCAIRE AND TARASCON

Beaucaire (pop 16,000) prospered as the site of an annual medieval trade fair. Its position near the lowest crossing point of the Rhone on trade routes linking Spain and Italy with France and accessible from the Mediterranean made it the largest commercial fair in southern Europe by the 17th century. The same amount of business was transacted in six days here as in one year in Marseille. A number of grand merchant's houses reflect the prosperity of the time. The fair lives on as a six-day festival (21 June–26 June) when Camargue black bulls are run through the streets in Spanish style.

Beaucaire and its sister town Tarascon across the river both have castles. Beaucaire's was built in 1180 for the Counts of Toulouse and was besieged and partly destroyed during the crusade against the Cathars (1209–1229). Rebuilt during the 14th century, it saw action during both the Hundred Years' War and the Wars of Religion. After it was occupied by rebels during a local uprising against the French government over taxation (1632), most of the castle was pulled down under the orders of Cardinal Richelieu. However, the keep, part of the walls and a chapel survived, and were made a listed monument in 1862. Tarascon castle, on the riverside facing Beaucaire, is altogether grander. Known as King René's Château after its builder in 1449, it is one of the best-preserved medieval castles in France. There are two parts: the southern part with its corner towers was a stately home for the Kings of Provence while the northern part was a military garrison.

At end of basin, fork L up ramp beside steps and turn L at top across canal bridge. At roundabout S of canal basin, go straight ahead (first exit, sp Fourques) then keep R at fork (Ave de la Plaine) and go ahead at crossroads and under railway bridge.

Turn R beside 14th-century Gothic-arch covered cross L then continue over irrigation canal and fork L (Ch de Beauvoir). Pass under road bridge and continue

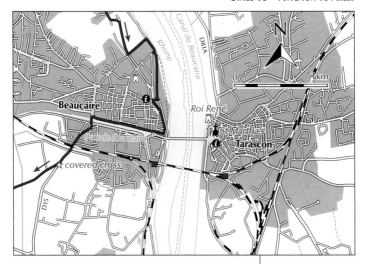

winding through fields and vineyards. Fork L by wayside cross and continue to T-junction beside **La Vieux Mas** (46.5km, 3m). ▸

Dog-leg R and L to continue on Ch de Beauvoir. Turn R at T-junction (Ch du Mas de Forton) and L (Ch de la Cabanette) winding through fields. Turn L at T-junction (Ch de Saujan) then first R (Ch du Petit Belleval). Turn R at next T-junction (Ch du Mas Maillan) and first L, then cross canal Philippe-Lamour. After 100m, turn R (Ch St Paul) and continue to T-junction. ▸ Turn L, then keep R (still Ch St Paul) at next fork. Pass under road bridge and through flood dyke to emerge on main road. Turn R, then go ahead at roundabout into **Fourques** (55km, 6m).

Pass car park L and where road ahead becomes one-way, turn L beside car park past old well and immediately R (Rue des Arènes). Follow this bearing L then turn R (Rue des Écoles) past church L. Follow this bearing L, then turn R on cycle track parallel with flood dyke. Bear half-L at crossroads (Rue de la Rompie) then turn sharply R uphill to reach roundabout. Go ahead (second exit) and cross old suspension bridge over Petit Rhône.

La Vieux Mas is a petting farm and traditional farming museum.

R turn at T-junction, waymarked ViaRhôna, leads to an alternative end point west along the coast at Sète.

227

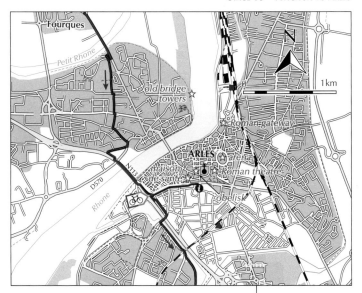

Continue ahead (Ave Edouard Herriot) for 125m then turn sharply R in front of house 67, back along roadside cycle track and dropping down to lower level. ▸ Follow cycle track, turning L and L again (Rue Robert Martin), following cycle track across road to R. Pass school entrance R, then dog-leg L and R under railway bridge and continue ahead (Ch de Dragées). Go ahead L (Rue Bracke Desrousseau) over staggered crossroads to reach T-junction. Turn L and immediately fork R (Ch de St Genest). At end, turn R and R again (Rue Jean Mattieu Artaud) then at end follow cycle track bearing L onto bridge over Rhone. On other side of river, descend ramp L of bridge to reach stage end at junction with Bvd Georges Clemenceau in **Arles** (58.5km, 8m) (accommodation, refreshments, youth hostel, tourist office, cycle shop, station). ▸

This sharp R turn is easy to miss.

To reach city centre, turn L on Bvd Clemenceau.

ARLES

The well-preserved Roman amphitheatre in Arles is used for concerts and bullfights

Arles (pop 51,000) was a Phoenician port before being captured by the Romans in 123BC. During the civil war Arles supported Julius Caesar against Pompey. This proved a good choice because, after he was victorious, Caesar raised the town to the status of *colonia* and endowed it with many formal buildings including an arena, triumphal arch, circus and theatre in addition to the normal range of forum, temples and baths. The city reached its heyday in the fourth century when it became Roman prefecture for all of France and Spain with a population of 100,000. It was further favoured by emperor Constantine, who built baths that are still standing. Arles was one of the first cities in Gaul to accept Christianity and it remained an important religious centre, rivalling Vienne, for hundreds of years. In AD855 it became a separate kingdom and remained so until 1239 when it was subsumed into Provence before becoming part of France in 1376.

Arles remained an important river port until the coming of the railway in 1847 diminished this trade. In 1888 the artist Vincent van Gogh moved to the town, attracted by the slower pace of life and fascinated by Provençale landscapes. Although he stayed only 15 months, he produced over 300 paintings during his time in Arles, including some of his best-known works. While in the city his mental health deteriorated, leading to him amputating his ear and eventually being confined to an asylum.

STAGE 20

Arles to Port-St Louis-du-Rhône

Start	Arles, Bvd Georges Clemenceau (8m)
Finish	Port-St Louis-du-Rhône, Tour St Louis (1m)
Distance	43km plus 7.5km to reach the sea
Waymarking	ViaRhôna V60A

The final stage follows a voie verte along canal towpaths and disused railway lines through open country. It crosses an area of salt flats, passing salt lakes and marshes with very little shade and in summer a considerable number of mosquitoes. Although the track is completely flat, it should not be taken lightly. Make sure you have a sun hat, sun protection cream and strong insect repellent.

This obelisk in Arles was brought from Egypt by the Romans

THE CAMARGUE

Camargue horses are free roaming

Near Arles the Rhone divides into two channels, Petit Rhône and Rhône. The low-lying land between them forms the Rhone delta, better known as the Camargue. This is a vast plain, one third of which is taken up with *étangs* (salt lakes) and *marais* (reed-covered marshes). The northern part has been developed as agricultural land, surrounded by dykes to keep the salt water out, where there are a number of large estates known vernacularly as *mas*. Towards the sea, large areas have been exploited as salt pans, originally by wealthy Cistercian 'salt-abbeys' but more recently by large chemical companies such as Solvay and Péchiney based in the salt 'mining' towns of Salin-de-Giraud and Aigues-Mortes. The Étang de Vaccarès (the largest étang) was made a nature park in 1927 and this has subsequently been expanded to cover a larger area. Animal life includes white horses and black cattle. Both are semi-feral, being allowed to roam and forage freely although owned by humans. The park is a haven for many bird species, particularly as a stop-over point on annual migrations. The most attractive and visible birds are flocks of greater flamingos. Cormorant colonies can be found around the étangs. One other creature is unfortunately abundant: the mosquito, the Camargue being home to some of the most virulent mosquitoes in France.

From Bvd Georges Clemenceau in **Arles**, follow cycle track S beside ruins of Carmes Déchaussés church L and continue past car park R. At end, bear R over motorway and cross bridge over Arles–Fos canal. Immediately after bridge, turn L on cycle track downhill then continue beside canal L on Quai Jean Boudignion. Pass under railway bridge and fork L (sp Pont van Gogh), still beside canal. Where road ends continue on cycle track beside canal. Emerge onto road (Rue Gaspard Monge) and bear L passing Pont de Langlois wooden lifting bridge L (2.5km, 4m). ▶

Pont de Langlois was the subject of four paintings by van Gogh and is popularly known as Pont van Gogh.

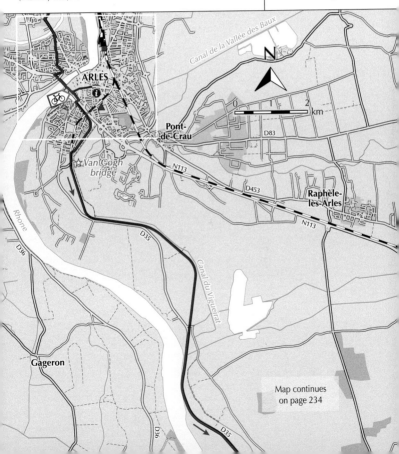

Map continues on page 234

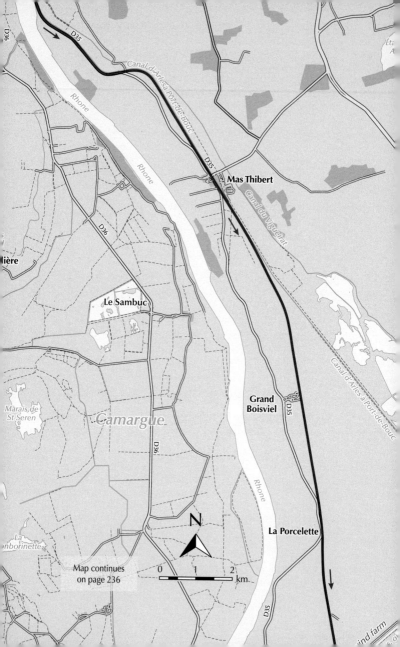

D36

D35

Canal d'Arles a Port-de-Bouc

Rhône

Rhône

D35

Mas Thibert

Canal du Vigueirat

D36

ière

Le Sambuc

Marais de
St Seren

Camargue

D36

Grand
Boisviel

D35

La Porcelette

La
nborinette

N

Map continues
on page 236

0   1   2
                 km

Rhône

D35

Canal d'Arles a Port-de-Bouc

nd farm

Bear L on cycle track beside canal and follow this winding through flat agricultural land for 16km to reach **Mas Thibert** (18.5km, 3m) (refreshments).

Continue on cycle track beside canal, eventually bearing gently R away from canal along course of old railway through vineyards planted on sand and rice paddies. Pass **Grand Boisviel** hamlet and **La Porcelette** (29km, 2m) both R and continue towards windfarm on horizon. Turn R by first turbine and dog-leg L and R past pumping station with Canal du Rhône à Fos L. Turn sharply R before next turbine, then sharply L alongside drainage ditch R. Pass final wind turbine then go ahead L at junction and fork R to join road (D35) over canal with **Barcarin** lock (34.5km, 4m) L. Immediately after bridge, fork L on cycle track that curves L then R to pass under road. Continue ahead, with road L and canal R, to reach Barcarin ferry.

Bear L beside ferry ramp and follow cycle track beside flood dyke R to reach beginning of Port-St Louis-du-Rhône. Go ahead over crossing of tracks, still following flood dyke now behind houses L. Follow white track alongside residential road and continue past more houses L. Bear R following winding track to reach riverbank. Turn L alongside Rhone and continue onto cycle track beside riverside road to reach end of stage at tourist office in castellated La Tour St Louis L on riverfront in **Port-St Louis-du-Rhône** (43km, 1m) (accommodation, refreshments, tourist office).

La Tour St Louis marks the end of the ViaRhôna

La Porcelette

Map continues
on page 239

km

D35

wind farm

Canal St Louis, ou Canal
du Rhône à Fos

☆ Barcarin lock

D268

D35

Rhone

N

0   1   2
km

Port-St-Louis-
du-Rhône

🚲 ℹ

Golfe de Fos

Napoléon marina

salt pans

*They de
Sainte-Ursule*

*Trou de
l'Oie*

*Grau de
Piémanson*

*Étang de
Grande Palun*

*Étang de
Napoléon*

Napoléon b

*Rhone
mouth*

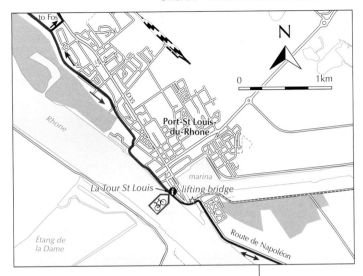

Port-St Louis-du-Rhône (pop 8500) is situated between the Rhone and the Golfe de Fos. Five thousand years ago the Rhone entered the Mediterranean here, but five millennia of deposition of sediment brought down by the river has pushed the mouth 7km south. The Tour St Louis was built in 1737 to control access to the Rhone from the sea. Development of the port and town began in 1871. The port has expanded into a large commercial harbour extending east around the Golfe de Fos and is managed as part of the port of Marseille. The town itself concentrates upon leisure craft and commercial fishing, with two well-equipped marinas.

You have reached the last town on the Rhone, but you have not reached the sea. It is another 7.5km by road across salt flats to the Mediterranean. Continue past La Tour, passing Rhone cruise boat landing stage R. Bear L on cycle track to join road (Rue Bonnardel) over blue

The very end of the road at Napoléon beach on the Mediterranean coast

lifting bridge (cycle track L) that crosses entrance to inner harbour. Turn R at roundabout (Ave Anatole France), parallel with river R. Continue onto Rte de Napoléon (cycle track R). Keep ahead at roundabout (first exit), where cycle track switches to L. Pass **Port Napoléon** marina L and continue straight across salt flats to reach small fishing community of St Louis beside the Golfe de Fos. Follow road ahead to reach sea at Napoléon beach (7.5km, 0m). Road and Rhone Cycle Route end here; to reach Rhone mouth (3.5km W) you can walk or cycle along beach, depending upon state of the tide. Otherwise, stop here and celebrate with a dip in the Med!

To reach Fos-sur-Mer station

The best way out of **Port-St Louis** is to catch cycle-carrying bus back to Arles station (see Getting there and back). If you want to cycle, nearest station is

Fos-sur-Mer, 27.5km E on other side of Golfe de Fos. To get there, retrace your route out of Port-St Louis-du-Rhône, then turn R at end of built-up area on cycle track between houses R and scrubland L. Turn L at T-junction (D268, sp Fos-sur-Mer) and continue across salt flats for 13.5km. Go ahead at three roundabouts, passing industrial areas R and crossing Canal St Louis. Bear R at fourth roundabout (N568) and follow this dual carriage-way (cycling on hard shoulder) for 10.5km, going ahead at two more roundabouts, passing oil refinery R and Fos Ville L. Continue following N568 bearing L alongside canal R and take small slip road R (sp Cimenterie). Bear R back under main road and turn R (first exit) at round-about. Fork immediately L (Ave de la Gare, sp Gare de Fos), then go ahead over mini-roundabout and turn L before railway bridge to reach **Fos** station R (27.5km).

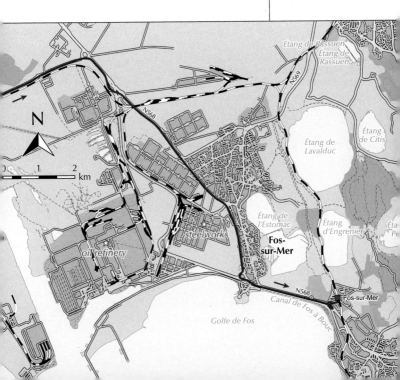

APPENDIX A
Facilities summary

	distance (km)	cumulative (km)	altitude (m)	accommodation	meals	hostels / gîtes	camping	tourist office	cycle shop	station
Prologue										
Andermatt			1456	x	x		x	x		x
Realp			1538	x	x					x
Furka Belvédère	(15)	15	2275		x					
Stage 1										
Gletsch	7.5	7.5	1762	x	x			x		x
Rhonequelle hotel				x	x					
Oberwald	6.5	14	1366	x	x			x	x	x
Obergesteln	2.5	16.5	1355	x	x					x
Wichel	1.5	18	1350	x	x		x			x
Geschinen										x
Münster	4.5	22.5	1335	x	x			x		x
Reckingen	2.5	25	1317	x	x		x	x		x
Ritzingen							x			x
Biel										x
Blitzingen	5.5	30.5	1257	x	x					x
Niederwald	1.5	32	1242		x					x
Mühlebach				x	x					
Ernen	6	38	1200	x	x			x		
Ausserbinn (variant)	(3.5)	(3.5)	1286	x	x					
Bächerhyschere (variant)				x	x					
Grengiols (variant)	(8)	(11.5)	1029	x	x					x
Filet (via variant)	(6.5)	(18)	760	x	x		x			
Lax	3	41	1042	x	x					x
Bettmeralp cable car	5	46	823				x			x
Filet	2.5	48.5	760	x	x		x			
Mörel	0.5	49	764	x	x				x	x
Bitsch										x
Naters (Brig off-route)	6.5	55.5	671	x	x		x	x	x	x

	distance (km)	cumulative (km)	altitude (m)	accommodation	meals	hostels / gîtes	camping	tourist office	cycle shop	station
Stage 2										
Brigerbad	6	61.5	652	x	x		x			
Lalden *(Eyholz off-route)*				x			x			x
Raron	11.5	73	638	x	x			x		x
Niedergestein					x					
Steg *(Gampel off-route)*	5	78	630	x	x		x			x
Gampinen				x	x					
Susten *(Leuk)*	9	87	632	x	x		x	x		x
Pfynwald							x			
Sierre/Siders	9.5	96.5	541	x	x		x	x	x	x
Stage 3										
Bramois *(Uvrier off-route)*	12	108.5	*504*	x	x		x		x	x
Sion	5.5	114	495	x	x	YH		x	x	x
Aproz	5.5	119.5	485		x		x			x
Riddes	8	127.5	476							x
Fully	10	137.5	465	x	x					
Branson	3.5	141	455	x						
Martigny (off-route)	(2.5)			x	x		x	x	x	x
Stage 4										
Vernayaz	5	146	454	x	x					x
Evionnaz	4	150	455							x
Lavey-les-Bains (off-route)				x	x					
St Maurice	5.5	155.5	419	x	x			x		x
Massongex *(Bex off-route)*	3.5	159	398	x	x				x	x
Monthey					x					x
Collombey					x					x
Illarsaz *(Aigle off-route)*	9.5	168.5	389	x	x			x		x
Vouvry	5	173.5	378	x	x					x
Le Bouveret	7.5	181	375	x	x		x	x		x
St Gingolph	4.5	185.5	384	x	x					x
Stage 5A										
Villeneuve	5	5	*374*	x	x		x	x		x

	distance (km)	cumulative (km)	altitude (m)	accommodation	meals	hostels / gîtes	camping	tourist office	cycle shop	station
Territet				x	x	YH				x
Montreux	5	10	384	x	x			x	x	x
Clarens				x	x					x
Burier							x			x
Vevey	7	17	379	x	x		x	x	x	x
Corsier-sur-Vevey				x	x					
Corseaux				x	x					x
St Saphorin	5	22	445	x	x					x
Chexbres	1.5	23.5	519	x	x			x		x
Epesses	3	26.5	465	x	x					x
Riex					x					
Cully				x	x		x	x		x
Grandvaux	3	29.5	492	x	x					x
Aran					x					
Lutry	3	32.5	380	x	x			x	x	x
Pully					x				x	x
Ouchy (Lausanne off-route)	4.5	37	374	x	x	YH	x	x	x	x
St Sulpice	7	44	397	x	x				x	
Préverenges				x	x					
Morges	6	50	373	x	x		x	x	x	x
Stage 6A										
St Prex	6	56	380	x	x			x		x
Buchillon	3	59	401		x					x
Allaman	2.5	61.5	405	x	x					x
Perroy	2.5	64	420		x					
Rolle	3	67	391	x	x		x	x		x
Gland	9	76	431	x	x					x
Prangins	3.5	79.5	418	x	x					x
Nyon	2.5	82	405	x	x			x	x	x
Crans-près-Céligny	5	87	426		x					
Céligny					x					
Founex				x	x					

	distance (km)	cumulative (km)	altitude (m)	accommodation	meals	hostels / gîtes	camping	tourist office	cycle shop	station
Coppet	5.5	92.5	395	x	x			x		x
Tannay				x	x		x			x
Mies				x	x					x
Versoix	6.5	99	388	x	x					x
Genthod										x
Bellevue	3.5	102.5	377	x	x					x
Geneva	5.5	108	374	x	x	YH		x	x	x
Stage 5										
Bret				x						
Meillerie	6.5	192	399	x	x					
Lugrin	5.5	197.5	380		x		x			
Grande Rive				x	x					
Évian-les-Bains	4.5	202	382	x	x	g		x		x
Amphion-les-Bains	5	207	380	x	x		x	x		
Vongy					x					
Thonon-les-Bains	7	214	381	x	x		x	x	x	x
Stage 6										
Corzent					x				x	
Anthy-sur-Léman	5	219	401	x	x		x		x	
Port de Séchex				x	x					
Songy	4	223	374		x		x			
Bonnatrait	1	224	402	x	x					
Sciez	2	226	399		x			x		
Excenevex	3.5	229.5	386	x	x		x	x		
Yvoire	3.5	233	388	x	x		x	x		
Nernier				x	x					
Messery	4	237	419	x	x		x	x		
Chens-sur-Léman	3.5	240.5	417		x		x			
Chens-le-Pont					x					
Hermance	3.5	244	375	x	x		x			
Vésenaz	9	253	421		x		x			
Les Eaux-Vives				x	x				x	x
Geneva	6.5	259.5	374	x	x	YH		x	x	x

	distance (km)	cumulative (km)	altitude (m)	accommodation	meals	hostels / gîtes	camping	tourist office	cycle shop	station
Stage 7										
Lancy				x	x					x
Onex	5.5	265	430	x	x					
Confignon				x	x					
Bernex	3	268	444		x					
Aire-la-Ville (Satigny off-route)	3.5	271.5	379		x		x			
Russin	3	274.5	420		x					x
La Plaine	2.5	277	354		x					x
Avully	1.5	278.5	425		x					
Chancy	4	282.5	364		x					x
Valleiry	5.5	288	464		x					x
Vulbens	4	292	484		x					
Clarafond	10	302	506		x					
Chêne-en-Semine	4.5	306.5	528		x					
Seyssel	12	318.5	258	x	x	g	x	x	x	x
Stage 8										
Châteaufort	4.5	323	294	x	x				x	
La Loi (Culoz off-route)	11.5	334.5	239		x	g	x	x	x	x
La Muraille (Vions off-route)				x	x					x
Chanaz	6.5	341	231	x	x	g	x	x		
Écoinçon					x					
Massignieu-de-Rives	6.5	347.5	235		x		x		x	
Belley (off-route)	5.5	353	232	x	x			x	x	x
Champagneux dam	18.5	371.5	211							
St Genix-sur-Guiers (off-route)	(5)		218	x	x		x	x		
Stage 9										
Cuchet					x					
La Bruyère	4	375.5	244		x		x			
Évieu	6.5	382	207		x					
Tours					x		x			
Brangues	10.5	392.5	218		x		x			

	distance (km)	cumulative (km)	altitude (m)	accommodation	meals	hostels / gîtes	camping	tourist office	cycle shop	station
Morestel	5.5	398	211	x	x		x	x	x	
Crévières	4	402	243	x						
l'Épaux					x					
Montalieu-Vercieu	19	421	205	x	x	g	x	x	x	
Sault-Brénaz	7.5	428.5	200	x	x		x			
Lagnieu	6	434.5	203	x	x				x	
Stage 10										
La-Balme-les-Grottes	4	438.5	208		x		x			
La Brosse	4.5	443	203				x			
Hières-sur-Amby	5.5	448.5	235	x	x		x			
Les Cinq Chemins	9.5	458	198	x	x					
Chavanoz					x					
Asnières					x					
Jons	14	472	204	x	x					
Jonage bridge	4.5	476.5	182	x	x					
Meyzieu bridge	4.5	481	180	x	x					
Pont d'Herbens					x		x			
Miribel-Jonage park	5.5	486.5	177		x					
Lyon	12.5	499	165	x	x	YH	x	x	x	x
Stage 11										
Oullins				x	x					x
Pierre-Bénite	7	506	169	x	x					x
Irigny					x					x
Vieux Port					x					
Vernaison	7	513	176	x	x					x
Givors	10.5	523.5	159	x	x				x	x
Loire-sur-Rhône	3.5	527	167		x					
Ste Colombe *(Vienne off-route)*	7.5	534.5	152	x	x			x	x	x
Stage 12										
St Cyr-sur-le-Rhône					x	x				
Ampuis	6.5	541	150	x	x				x	
Tupin-et-Semons					x					

	distance (km)	cumulative (km)	altitude (m)	accommodation	meals	hostels / gîtes	camping	tourist office	cycle shop	station
Condrieu	6	547	145	x	x		x	x	x	
La Maladière				x	x					
Chavanay	6	553	142	x	x	g			x	
St Pierre-de-Bœuf	5.5	558.5	139		x	g	x		x	
Sablons (*Serrières off-route*)	9	567.5	139	x	x			x		
Stage 13										
St Rambert-d'Albon	5	572.5	135		x		x			x
Andancette	6.5	579	131	x	x					
Laveyron	5	584	130		x					
St Vallier/Sarras	2	586	127	x	x				x	x
Vion				x			x			
Tournon/Tain l'Hermitage	17.5	603.5	125	x	x	g	x	x	x	x
Stage 14										
La Roche-de-Glun	9	612.5	117		x		x			
Pont-de-l'Isère	4	616.5	117	x	x					
Bourg-lès-Valence	9	625.5	111	x	x					
Valence	2	627.5	128	x	x	g	x	x	x	x
Stage 15										
Pont de l'Epervière				x	x		x			
Soyons	10	637.5	108	x	x					
Charmes-sur-Rhône	4	641.5	109	x	x		x			
La Voulte-sur-Rhône	12	653.5	93	x	x			x		
Le Pouzin	7.5	661	92	x	x					
Stage 16										
Baix	7	668	97	x	x					
Cruas	7	675	83		x		x	x		
Rochemaure	11.5	686.5	72	x	x					
Pracomtal bridge	4.5	691	73							
Montélimar (off-route)	(3)			x	x			x	x	x

	distance (km)	cumulative (km)	altitude (m)	accommodation	meals	hostels / gîtes	camping	tourist office	cycle shop	station
Stage 17										
Châteauneuf-du-Rhône (off-route)				x	x		x			
Viviers	10.5	701.5	65	x	x		x	x		
Bourg-St Andéol	16	717.5	54	x	x		x	x		
Lapalud	8.5	726	45	x	x		x			
Le Bout-du-Pont	6	732	43	x						
Pont-St Esprit (off-route)				x	x	g	x	x		
Stage 18										
Mondragon	5.5	737.5	42	x	x					
Mornas	5.5	743	35	x	x					
Caderousse	15.5	758.5	29	x	x					
Sorgues	17	775.5	23	x	x		x			x
Le Pontet	6.5	782	22	x	x		x		x	
Avignon	6.5	788.5	19	x	x	YH	x	x	x	x
Stage 19										
Villeneuve-lez-Avignon				x	x	YH	x	x		
Les Angles	3.5	792	22	x						
Aramon	12.5	804.5	15	x	x			x		
Théziers	5	809.5	10	x						
Montfrin	6	815.5	12	x	x					
Beaucaire	11.5	827	5	x	x			x		x
Arles	20	847	8	x	x	YH		x	x	x
Stage 20										
Mas Thibert	18.5	865.5	3		x					
Port-St Louis-du-Rhône	24.5	890	1	x	x			x		

APPENDIX B
Tourist information offices

Stage 1
Andermatt
Gotthardstrasse 2, 6490
tel +41 41 888 71 00
www.andermatt.ch

Gletsch (late Jun–end Sep)
Furkastrasse, 3999
tel +41 27 973 14 90
www.infopoint-gletsch.ch

Oberwald
Dorfstrasse 5, 3999
tel +41 27 974 68 60
www.obergoms.ch

Münster
Furkastrasse 617, 3985
tel +41 27 974 68 68
www.obergoms.ch

Reckingen
Wiesenstrasse 27, 3998
tel +41 27 974 68 66
www.obergoms.ch

Ernen
Hengert 17, 3995
tel +41 27 971 50 55
www.landschaftspark-binntal.ch

Mörel-Filet
Furkastrasse 39, 3983
tel +41 27 928 58 58
www.aletscharena.ch

Brig
Bahnhofplatz 2, 3900
tel +41 27 921 60 30
www.brig-simplon.ch

Stage 2
Visp
Balfrinstrasse 3, 3930
tel +41 27 946 18 18
www.vispinfo.ch

Raron
Bahnhofstrasse 16, 3942
tel +41 27 934 31 00
www.loetschberg-region.ch

Leuk (Susten)
Bahnhofstrasse 6, 3952
tel +41 27 473 10 94
www.leuk.ch/tourismus

Sierre/Siders
Pl de la Gare 10, 3960
tel +41 27 455 85 35
www.sierretourisme.ch

Stage 3
Sion
Pl de la Planta 2, 1950
tel +41 27 327 77 27
www.siontourisme.ch

Martigny
Ave de la Gare 6, 1920
tel +41 27 720 49 49
www.martigny.com

Stage 4
St Maurice
Ave des Terreaux 1, 1890
tel +41 24 485 40 40
www.saint-maurice.ch

Aigle
Pl du Marché 2,1860
tel +41 24 466 30 00
www.aigle-tourisme.ch

Le Bouveret
Rue du Tonkin 2, 1897
tel +41 24 481 51 21
www.bouveret.ch

Stage 5
Évian-les-Bains
Pl de la porte d'Allinges 74500
tel +33 4 50 75 04 26
www.evian-tourisme.com

Publier-Amphion
Plage municipale d'Amphion 74500
tel +33 4 50 70 00 03
www.publier-tourisme.com

Thonon-les-Bains
2 Rue Michaud, 74200
tel +33 4 50 71 55 55
www.thononlesbains.com

Stage 6
Sciez
513 Ave de Sciez 74140
tel +33 4 50 72 64 57
www.destination-leman.com

Excenevex
138 Rue de Centre, 74140
tel +33 4 50 72 80 21
www.destination-leman.com

Yvoire
3 Pl de Mairie, 74140
tel +33 4 50 72 80 21
www.destination-leman.com

Messery
1 Ch de la Cure 74140
tel +33 4 50 94 75 55

Geneva
Quai du Mont-Blanc 1, 1201
tel +41 22 909 70 00
www.geneve.com

Stage 5A
Villeneuve
Pl de la Gare 5, 1844
tel +41 84 886 84 84
www.montreuxriviera.com

Montreux
Grande Rue 45 1820
tel +41 84 886 84 84
www.montreuxriviera.com

Vevey
Grande-Place 29, 1800
tel +41 84 886 84 84
www.montreuxriviera.com

Chexbres
Pl de la Gare, 1071
tel +41 84 886 84 84
www.montreuxriviera.com

Cully
Pl de la Gare 4, 1096
tel +41 84 886 84 84
www.montreuxriviera.com

Lutry
Pl des Halles 3, 1095
tel +41 84 886 84 84
www.montreuxriviera.com

Ouchy
Pl de la Navigation 6, 1006
tel +41 21 613 73 73
www.lausanne-tourisme.ch

Lausanne station
Pl de la Gare 9, 1003
tel +41 21 613 73 73
www.lausanne-tourisme.ch

Lausanne
Pl de la Cathédràle, 1014
tel +41 21 613 73 73
www.lausanne-tourisme.ch

Morges
Rue du Château 2, 1110
tel +41 21 801 32 33
www.morges-tourisme.ch

Stage 6A
St Prex
Pl de l'Horloge, 1162
tel +41 21 806 50 26
www.saint-prex.ch

Rolle
Grand-Rue 1bis, 1180
tel +41 21 825 15 35
www.tourisme-rolle.ch

Nyon
Ave Viollier 8, 1260
tel +41 22 365 66 00
www.lacote-tourisme.ch

Coppet
Grand-Rue 65, 1296
tel +41 22 960 87 37
www.lacote-tourisme.ch

Stage 7
Seyssel
10 Rte d'Aix-les-Bains 74910
tel +33 4 76 89 05 78
www.ot-pays-de-seyssel.fr

Stage 8
Culoz (Jun–Sep)
La Maison du vélo,
Rue du Stade, 01350
tel +33 4 79 81 29 06
www.bugeysud-tourisme.fr

Chanaz
Pl Antoine Gianetto, 73310

tel +33 4 79 88 68 00
www.chanaz.fr

Belley
34 Grande Rue, 01300
tel +33 4 79 81 29 06
www.bugeysud-tourisme.fr

St Genix-sur-Guiers
47 Rte de Pont de Beauvoisin 73240
tel +33 4 79 36 00 02
www.pays-lac-aiguebelette.com

Stage 9
Morestel
100 Pl des Halles 38510
tel +33 4 74 80 19 59
www.tousauxbalcons.com

Montalieu-Vercieu
5 Pl de la Mairie 38390
tel +33 4 74 88 48 56
www.valleebleue.org

Stage 10
Lyon
Pl Bellecour, 69214
tel +33 4 72 77 69 69
www.lyon-france.com

Stage 11
St Romain-en-Gal
Musée Gallo-Romain D502, 69560
tel +33 4 74 57 33 71
www.vienne-condrieu.com

Vienne
14 Cours Brillier, 38200
tel +33 4 74 53 70 10
www.vienne-condrieu.com

Stage 12
Condrieu
Pl du Séquoïa, 69420
tel +33 4 74 56 62 83
www.vienne-condrieu.com

Serrières
Quai Jules Roche Sud, 07340
tel +33 4 75 34 06 01
www.ardechegrandair.com

Stage 13
Tournon-sur-Rhône
2 Pl St Julien, 07300
tel +33 4 75 08 10 23
www.ardeche-hermitage.com

Tain-l'Hermitage
Pl du 8 Mai 1945, 26601
tel +33 4 75 08 10 23
www.ardeche-hermitage.com

Stage 14
Valence
11 Bvd Bancel, 26000
tel +33 4 75 44 90 40
www.valence-romans-tourisme.com

Stage 15
La Voulte-sur-Rhône
Pl Étienne Jargeat, 07800
tel +33 4 75 20 81 81
www.ardeche-buissonniere.fr

Stage 16
Cruas
1 Pl de la Liberté, 07250
tel +33 4 75 49 59 20
www.sud-ardeche-tourisme.com

Montélimar
Espace St Martin, 26200
tel +33 4 75 01 00 20
www.montelimar-tourisme.com

Stage 17
Viviers
2 Ave Mendès France, 07220
tel +33 4 75 54 54 20
www.rhone-gorges-ardeche.com

Bourg-St Andéol
Pl du Champ de Mars, 07700
tel +33 4 75 54 54 20
www.rhone-gorges-ardeche.com

Pont-St Esprit
162 Ave Kennedy, 30130
tel +33 4 66 39 44 45
www.provenceoccitane.com

Stage 18
Avignon
41 Cours Jean Jaurès, 84004
tel +33 4 32 74 32 74
www.avignon-tourisme.com

Stage 19
Villeneuve-lez-Avignon
Pl Charles David, 30400
tel +33 4 90 03 70 60
www.avignon-tourisme.com

Aramon
Pl. Ledru Rollin, 30390
tel +33 4 66 22 68 88
www.uzes-pontdugard.com

Beaucaire
8 Rue Victor Hugo, 30300
tel +33 4 66 59 26 57
www.provence-camargue-tourisme.com

Tarascon
62 Rue des Halles,13150
tel +33 4 90 91 03 52
www.tarascon.org

Arles
9 Bvd des Lices, 13200
tel +33 4 90 18 41 20
www.arlestourisme.com

Stage 20
Port-St Louis-du-Rhône
La Tour St Louis Quai Bonnardel, 13230
tel +33 4 42 86 01 21
www.portsaintlouis-tourisme.fr

APPENDIX C
Youth hostels and gîtes d'étape

Youth hostels

Stage 3
Sion (86 beds)
Rue de l'Industrie 2
Sion (VS) 1950
tel +41 27 323 74 70

Stage 5A
Montreux (Territet) (112 beds)
Passage de l'Auberge 8
Montreux-Territet (VD) 1820
tel +41 21 963 49 34

Lausanne (320 beds)
Ch du Bois-de-Vaux 36
Lausanne (VD) 1007
tel +41 21 626 02 22

Stage 6/6A
Geneva (private) (334 beds)
Rue Rothschild 28
Genève (GE) 1202
tel +41 22 732 62 60

Stage 10
Lyon FUAJ (180 beds)
41–45 Montée du Chemin Neuf
Lyon 69005
tel +33 4 78 15 05 50

Stage 18
Avignon (private) (141 beds)
Camping Bagatelle
25 Allée Antoine Pinay
Ile de la Barthelasse
Avignon 84000
tel +33 4 90 86 30 39

Stage 19
Villeneuve-lez-Avignon (YMCA)
(140 beds)
7bis Chemin de la Justice
Villeneuve-lez-Avignon 30400
tel +33 4 90 25 46 20

Arles (FUAJ) (110 beds)
20 Ave Foch
Arles 13200
tel +33 4 90 96 31 26

Gîtes d'étape

Stage 5
Évian-les-Bains (72 beds)
31 Ave de Neuvecelle
Évian 74501
tel +33 4 50 75 35 87

Stage 7
Seyssel (52 beds)
l'Edelweiss, Les Côtes-d'en-Haut
478 Rte de La Praz
Seyssel 74910
tel +33 4 50 56 04 75

Stage 8
Culoz (15 beds)
Le Cabiolon
2–8 Rue de Chantemerle
Culoz 01350
tel +33 4 79 87 00 29.

Chanaz (10 beds)
89 Montée du Fort
Chanaz 73310
tel +33 4 79 35 16 32

Stage 9
Montalieu-Vercieu (14 beds)
Base de Loisirs de la Vallée Bleue
Montalieu-Vercieu 38390
tel +33 4 74 88 63 67

Stage 12
Chavanay (15 beds)
1 Rue de l'Ancienne Cure
Chavanay 42410
tel +33 7 81 34 64 64

St Pierre-de-Bœuf (11 beds)
Maison de la Lône
8 Ave du Rhône
St Pierre-de-Bœuf 42520
tel +33 4 69 32 47 47

Stage 13
Tournon-sur-Rhône (15 beds)
Le Pied du Géant
25 Grande Rue
Tournon 07300
tel +33 06 75 37 44 05

Stage 14
Valence (10 beds)
VéloGite Valence
11 Allée des Petits Champs
Valence 26000
tel +33 4 75 80 53 43

Stage 17
Pont-St Esprit (14 beds)
122 Passage Pont d'Ardèche
Pont-St Esprit 30130
tel +33 4 66 39 29 80

APPENDIX D
Useful contacts

Transportation
Eurostar
tel 0343 218 6186 (reservations)
tel 0344 822 5822 (baggage)
EuroDespatch@eurostar.com (baggage)
www.eurostar.com

SNCF (French railways)
tel +33 1 84 94 36 35
(just 3635 within France)
www.sncf-connect.com

SBB/CFF (Swiss railways)
www.sbb.ch

The man in seat 61
(European rail travel advice)
www.seat61.com

European Bike Express
tel 0143 042 2111
info@bike-express.co.uk
www.bike-express.co.uk

PostAuto Schweiz (Andermatt–
Furkapass–Oberwald bus)
Region Bern/Zentralalpen
tel +41 58 448 20 08
www.postauto.ch/bern

Zou (Port-St Louis–Arles bus)
tel +33 4 42 55 83 19
www.zou.maregionsud.fr

Excess Baggage Company
(bike boxes at London airports)
www.left-baggage.co.uk

Accommodation
Youth Hostels Association
tel 0800 019 1700
customerservices@yha.org.uk
www.yha.org.uk

Hostelling International
(youth hostel bookings)
www.hihostels.com

Gîtes d'étape guide
www.gites-refuges.com

Cycling organisations
Cycling UK
(formerly Cyclists' Touring Club)
Parklands, Railton Rd
Guildford GU2 9JX
tel 0148 323 8301 (membership)
tel 0844 736 8458 (insurance)
www.cyclinguk.org

Maps and guides
Swiss route guide (click on 'National
routes' then 'Rhone route')
www.veloland.ch

French route guide
www.viarhona.com

Open Street Maps (online mapping)
www.openstreetmap.org

Stanfords
7 Mercer Walk
London WC2H 9AF
tel 0207 836 1321
sales@stanfords.co.uk
www.stanfords.co.uk

The Map Shop
15 High St
Upton upon Severn, Worcs
WR8 0HJ
tel 0800 085 4080 or 0168 459 3146
themapshop@btinternet.com
www.themapshop.co.uk

APPENDIX E
Language glossary

English	French	German
yes	*oui*	*ja*
no	*non*	*nein*
please	*s'il vous plaît*	*bitte*
thank you	*merci*	*danke schön*
abbey	*l'abbaye (f)*	*das Kloster*
barrier	*la barrière*	*die Schranke*
bicycle	*le vélo*	*das Fahrrad*
brake	*le frein*	*die Bremse*
bridge	*le pont*	*die Brücke*
castle	*le château*	*das Schloss/die Burg*
cathedral	*la cathédrale*	*die Dom*
church	*l'église (f)*	*die Kirche*
county	*le département*	*der Kanton*
cycle track	*la véloroute*	*der Radweg*
cyclist	*le cycliste*	*der Radfahrer*
dam	*le barrage*	*der Damm*
diversion	*le déviation*	*die Umleitung*
dyke	*la levée*	*der Deich*
ferry	*le bac*	*die Fähre*
field	*le champ*	*das Feld*
flood	*l'inondation (f)*	*das Hochwasser*
forest/woods	*la forêt/les bois*	*der Wald/der Wald*
fort	*le fort*	*die Festung*
lock	*l'écluse (f)*	*die Schleuse*

English	French	German
monastery	le monastère	das Kloster
monument	le monument	die Denkmal
motorway	l'autoroute (f)	die Autobahn
no entry	entrée interdite	einfahrt verboten
one-way street	sens unique	die Einbahnstrasse
puncture	la crevaison	der Reifenpanne
railway	le chemin de fer	die (Eisen)bahn
river	la fleuve	der Fluss
riverbank	le rive	das Ufer
road closed	route fermée	Strasse gesperrt
station	la gare	der Bahnhof
tourist information office	l'office de tourisme (m)	das Fremdenverkehrsbüro
town hall/city hall	la mairie/l'hôtel de ville (f)	das Rathaus
youth hostel	l'auberge de jeunesse (f)	die Jugendherberge

NOTES

NOTES

Lyon has many kilometres of quayside along the Rhone and Saône (Stage 10)

DOWNLOAD THE ROUTES IN GPX FORMAT

All the routes in this guide are available for download from:

www.cicerone.co.uk/1082/GPX

as standard format GPX files. You should be able to load them into most online GPX systems and mobile devices, whether GPS or smartphone. You may need to convert the file into your preferred format using a conversion programme such as gpsvisualizer.com or one of the many other such websites and programmes.

When you follow this link, you will be asked for your email address and where you purchased the guidebook, and have the option to subscribe to the Cicerone e-newsletter.

www.cicerone.co.uk

LISTING OF CICERONE GUIDES

BRITISH ISLES CHALLENGES, COLLECTIONS AND ACTIVITIES

Cycling Land's End to John o' Groats
Great Walks on the England Coast Path
The Big Rounds
The Book of the Bivvy
The Book of the Bothy
The Mountains of England & Wales:
  Vol 1 Wales
  Vol 2 England
The National Trails
Walking The End to End Trail

SCOTLAND

Ben Nevis and Glen Coe
Cycle Touring in Northern Scotland
Cycling in the Hebrides
Great Mountain Days in Scotland
Mountain Biking in Southern and Central Scotland
Mountain Biking in West and North West Scotland
Not the West Highland Way Scotland
Scotland's Mountain Ridges
Scottish Wild Country Backpacking
Skye's Cuillin Ridge Traverse
The Borders Abbeys Way
The Great Glen Way
The Great Glen Way Map Booklet
The Hebridean Way
The Hebrides
The Isle of Mull
The Isle of Skye
The Skye Trail
The Southern Upland Way
The Speyside Way
The Speyside Way Map Booklet
The West Highland Way
The West Highland Way Map Booklet
Walking Ben Lawers, Rannoch and Atholl
Walking in the Cairngorms
Walking in the Pentland Hills
Walking in the Scottish Borders
Walking in the Southern Uplands
Walking in Torridon, Fisherfield, Fannichs and An Teallach
Walking Loch Lomond and the Trossachs
Walking on Arran
Walking on Harris and Lewis
Walking on Jura, Islay and Colonsay
Walking on Rum and the Small Isles
Walking on the Orkney and Shetland Isles
Walking on Uist and Barra
Walking the Cape Wrath Trail

Walking the Corbetts
  Vol 1 South of the Great Glen
  Vol 2 North of the Great Glen
Walking the Galloway Hills
Walking the Munros
  Vol 1 – Southern, Central and Western Highlands
  Vol 2 – Northern Highlands and the Cairngorms
Winter Climbs Ben Nevis and Glen Coe

NORTHERN ENGLAND ROUTES

Cycling the Reivers Route
Cycling the Way of the Roses
Hadrian's Cycleway
Hadrian's Wall Path
Hadrian's Wall Path Map Booklet
The C2C Cycle Route
The Coast to Coast Map Booklet
The Coast to Coast Walk
The Pennine Way
The Pennine Way Map Booklet
Walking the Dales Way
Walking the Dales Way Map Booklet

NORTH-EAST ENGLAND, YORKSHIRE DALES AND PENNINES

Cycling in the Yorkshire Dales
Great Mountain Days in the Pennines
Mountain Biking in the Yorkshire Dales
St Oswald's Way and St Cuthbert's Way
The Cleveland Way and the Yorkshire Wolds Way
The Cleveland Way Map Booklet
The North York Moors
The Reivers Way
Trail and Fell Running in the Yorkshire Dales
Walking in County Durham
Walking in Northumberland
Walking in the North Pennines
Walking in the Yorkshire Dales: North and East
Walking in the Yorkshire Dales: South and West

NORTH-WEST ENGLAND AND THE ISLE OF MAN

Cycling the Pennine Bridleway
Isle of Man Coastal Path
The Lancashire Cycleway
The Lune Valley and Howgills
Walking in Cumbria's Eden Valley
Walking in Lancashire

Walking in the Forest of Bowland and Pendle
Walking on the Isle of Man
Walking on the West Pennine Moors
Walks in Silverdale and Arnside

LAKE DISTRICT

Cycling in the Lake District
Great Mountain Days in the Lake District
Joss Naylor's Lakes, Meres and Waters of the Lake District
Lake District Winter Climbs
Lake District: High Level and Fell Walks
Lake District: Low Level and Lake Walks
Mountain Biking in the Lake District
Outdoor Adventures with Children – Lake District
Scrambles in the Lake District – North
Scrambles in the Lake District – South
Trail and Fell Running in the Lake District
Walking The Cumbria Way
Walking the Lake District Fells –
  Borrowdale
  Buttermere
  Coniston
  Keswick
  Langdale
  Mardale and the Far East
  Patterdale
  Wasdale
Walking the Tour of the Lake District

DERBYSHIRE, PEAK DISTRICT AND MIDLANDS

Cycling in the Peak District
Dark Peak Walks
Scrambles in the Dark Peak
Walking in Derbyshire
Walking in the Peak District – White Peak East
Walking in the Peak District – White Peak West

SOUTHERN ENGLAND

20 Classic Sportive Rides in South East England
20 Classic Sportive Rides in South West England
Cycling in the Cotswolds
Mountain Biking on the North Downs
Mountain Biking on the South Downs

CICERONE

**Trust Cicerone to guide your next adventure,
wherever it may be around the world...**

Discover guides for hiking, mountain walking, backpacking,
trekking, trail running, cycling and mountain biking, ski touring,
climbing and scrambling in Britain, Europe and worldwide.

Connect with Cicerone online and find inspiration.

- buy books and ebooks
- articles, advice and trip reports
- podcasts and live events
- GPX files and updates
- regular newsletter

cicerone.co.uk